The Humanity of Christ and the Healing of the Dysfunction of the Human Spirit

The Humanity of Christ and the Healing of the Dysfunction of the Human Spirit

Donald L. Alexander

WIPF & STOCK · Eugene, Oregon

THE HUMANITY OF CHRIST AND THE HEALING OF THE DYSFUNCTION OF THE HUMAN SPIRIT

Copyright © 2015 Donald L. Alexander. All rights reserved. Except for brief quotations in critical publications or reviews, no part of this book may be reproduced in any manner without prior written permission from the publisher. Write: Permissions, Wipf and Stock Publishers, 199 W. 8th Ave., Suite 3, Eugene, OR 97401.

Wipf & Stock
An Imprint of Wipf and Stock Publishers
199 W. 8th Ave., Suite 3
Eugene, OR 97401

www.wipfandstock.com

ISBN 13: 978-1-4982-0667-9

Manufactured in the U.S.A.   08/03/2015

Unless otherwise noted, Scripture verses are take from the Holy Bible, New International Version®, NIV® Copyright © 1973, 1978, 1984, 2011 by Biblica, Inc.® Used by permission. All rights reserved worldwide.

Of the many persons who have contributed to the thoughts and interpretations developed within this book, there are two persons to whom special recognition and thanks are due. These two persons have been a continued source of encouragement and help. They are distinguished scholars and embody in their personal lives the thesis of this book; that is, they exhibit a Christ-like character demonstrated in their cruciform love for others in their personal, spiritual, and social needs.

Dr. K. K. Yeo: Professor Yeo is Harry R. Kendall Professor of the New Testament at Garrett-Evangelical Seminary, Affiliate Faculty of the Department of Asian Languages and Cultures at Northwestern University, and a visiting professor of Peking University and Fudan University.

Dr. Mark Reasoner: Dr. Reasoner is associate professor of Christian theology and New Testament studies at Marian University, Indianapolis, Indiana.

Contents

Preface | ix
Introduction | xi
Acknowledgments | xv

1. Setting the Context: The Problem, Focus, and Thesis | 1
2. The Nature and Function of the Human Spirit | 29
3. The Dysfunction of the Human Spirit | 48
4. The Healing of the Dysfunction of the Human Spirit | 78
5. The Fruit of the Spirit: The Ultimate Goal of the Holy Spirit's Restoration | 106

Epilogue: Biblical Holiness as a Relational Concept | 110

Bibliography | 125
Index of Authors | 131
index of Subjects | 133

Preface

THIS BOOK REPRESENTS A personal quest in what Anselm referred to as *faith seeking understanding*. It began as a result of the course I had the privilege of teaching at Bethel University, St. Paul, Minnesota, entitled *Holiness in Biblical Perspective*. During the teaching of the class, the issue of the relationship of the human spirit to the divine Spirit arose. Since the overarching focus of the course centered on developing a compelling and consistent theology of the Christian life, the subject of sanctification/holiness of life was also central. Hence, the dual emphasis on spirituality and its relationship to a mature spiritual life created a genuine concern about living the Christian life in this present world. In addition, the relationship between the human spirit and the Holy Spirit continued to persist. Upon retirement from Bethel University and having time for reflection, I undertook the task to find some answers that would in turn provide a clearer grasp of the nature and purpose of redemption and that would also assist in a greater understanding of the development of a mature and sustain spiritual life.

The book aims at offering an interpretation of the nature and function of the human spirit for developing a theologically meaningful understanding of the relationship between the human spirit and the divine Spirit that would also offer a better understanding of the development of a mature spiritual life. To accomplish this purpose, it was necessary to offer a compelling theological-biblical interpretation of the nature and function of the human spirit and its relationship to the divine Spirit. The foundational premise

Preface

resides in the proposal that the core capacity of the human spirit resides in the ability for *self-relatedness*. It is this ability that enables humans to engage in personal relationship with the divine Spirit on the basis of Christ's redemptive work.

Introduction

THE CREATION OF ANY book is rarely the result of one person's single intellectual creativity. This is clearly the case in this book. There are many who have contributed over the years to the ideas and interpretations offered. The book in essence, however, represents my personal *faith seeking understanding* and is not intended to persuade.

It is impossible to thank all persons who helped to formulate the thoughts and interpretations contained in this book. The book is not intended to be an original treatise, but simply a personal interpretation of the role of human spirit and its relationship and significance for living the Christian life. Hopefully the book will create dialogue among teachers who study the spirituality of the New Testament or the general topic of Christian spirituality. I would, however, mention four authors whose writings and interpretations have made a significant contribution to the formulation of my thought. These authors are James E. Loder, Thomas F. Torrance (and his excellent expositor Elmer M. Colyer), Ray S. Anderson, and Warren S. Brown. Anyone familiar with the writings and interpretations advanced by these scholars will easily see their impact within the pages of this book.

A brief summary of the key concepts undergirding the thesis of the book hopefully will provide insight into the focus of the book as well as create some interest in the topic. The key concepts are as follows.

Introduction

The thesis of the book centers on the proposal that the human spirit is theologically significant both in a person's initial encounter with God and in the continued spiritual maturing of a believer's life. Several premises undergird the development of this proposal:

1. The ultimate goal of redemption points beyond forgiveness, though not independent of it, and centers on the restoration of the image of God in believers.
2. Apart from the human spirit the divine Spirit is personally unknowable.
3. The human spirit constitutes a unique *capacity* within human nature that enables human persons to engage in personal relatedness that in depth and complexity exceed that of our nearest creaturely companions.
4. As a result of humanity's idolatrous displacement of God the Creator, placing trust in creation and its creatures, humanity lost its capacity to function as persons created in the divine image of God.
5. The introduction of the phrase *dysfunction of the human spirit* is my synonym for the concept of the *sinful nature*.
6. The human spirit enables the functioning of the image of God within human nature.
7. Separated from its ground in the divine Spirit, the human spirit becomes dysfunctional, reversing its original exocentric capacity (to love, honor, and worship God and to love one's neighbor as oneself) to an egocentric outlook that vitalizes and empowers human perversity.
8. When restored to its original ground in the divine Spirit, the human spirit is called out of its futility and perversity into the light and truth of the divine Spirit, where and only where, it can be true to itself without losing its distinctive nature as human spirit (James Loder).
9. The work of the divine Spirit centers on the restoration of those virtues or character traits that originally marked

Introduction

humans as being in the image of God; that is, on becoming authentically human again according to the purpose for which God originally created humans.

10. The theological writings of the Protestant Evangelical church historically have neglected the subject of the human spirit, due to the assumption that any attempt to give a role to the human spirit in the experience of salvation is an attempt to bypass grace alone.

11. Sanctification (holiness) or spirituality is not something we achieve in the ordinary sense, such as, a violinist achieve proficiency on the violin, but something we become. It is to bear in our lives the imprint of the transforming work of the divine Spirit (Robert C. Roberts).

12. The divine Spirit and the human spirit were never intended by God to be mutually exclusive in relationship.

13. A fundamental interpretative premise resides in the conviction that the human spirit and the divine Spirit are made for each other according to the relationality ultimate designed to replicate the relationality of the divine and human in the person of Jesus Christ (James Loder).

Hyatt Moore, when writing a caption under the picture of an East Asian man in the book *In the Image of God: Faces and Souls That Reflect Their Creator*, comments, not purposefully but insightfully, on the relationship between creaturely existence and the uniqueness of the human spirit that unconsciously expresses the perspective of this book. Moore writes,

> There's a spirit within us. And that spirit is apparent in every baby, every child, every old man and woman. It's the essence of life that was first breathed into the first human and has continued ever since. It's not flesh that makes us who we are, nor bone, nor brain, nor throbbing heart. We're made in God's likeness, yet He is hardly comprised of such. The flesh will fade. The heart will stop; the

Introduction

blood that carries life will cease its faithful flowing. But the spirit that's within, that is something else again.[1]

---

1. Moore, *In the Image of God*, 64.

Acknowledgments

I WISH TO EXPRESS my thanks to the editors at University Press of America for permission to copy material from my former book *The Pursuit of Godliness: Sanctification in Christological Perspective*. Also to extend thanks to Hyatt Moore of Wycliffe Bible Translators for permission to copy his subscript from the remarkable book *In the Image of God: Faces and Souls That Reflect Their Creator*, containing extra-ordinary pictures, paintings, and sketches of the faces of people from Asia, Africa and the Middle East. Thanks and gratitude are also to be extended to my daughter, Karin, who took the time to assist me with some of the demands necessary to present a properly formatted manuscript, as my computer skills are greatly lacking. Special thanks and gratitude to my personal friend and former co-pastor Timothy Anderson. Pastor Anderson has been a dialogue partner, discussing theological-biblical issues and ideas about the Christian faith and the purpose of the Christian church. His insights and observations have been not only helpful but he has also been an encouraging friend to whom I owe him a debt of gratitude. Enormous thanks and gratitude are to be extended to my wife, Judy, who proofread the entire manuscript, correcting many typing errors, checking footnotes, and any grammatical errors, including an examination of consistency in footnotes and logic of argument. Finally, but not least, is gratitude expressed to my longtime friend Dr. Wendell Nelson, who has been an thoughtful and encouraging friend.

1

Setting the Context
The Problem, Focus, and Thesis

PROTESTANT EVANGELICAL CHRISTIANS HAVE developed little or no positive theological perception of the significance of the *human spirit* either in initial relationship with God or in the development of a spiritually mature Christian life. This lack is due in part to the de-spiriting of the human person within Protestant Evangelical theology. *Grace alone* has dominated the interpretation of salvation so that any movement on the part of the human spirit is viewed as an attempt to bypass *grace alone*. In this study, I will argue that the human spirit performs a significant role in both the Christian's initial relationship with God and in the healing (sanctification) of human nature.

Renewed interest in the significance of the human spirit and its relation to the divine Spirit and the Christian life occurred for me as a result of reading a chapter written by neurologist Warren S. Brown, "Cognitive Contributions to Soul," in the book he coauthored with Nancy Murphy and H. Newton Malony—namely, *Whatever Happened to the Soul? Scientific and Theological Portraits of Human Nature*—and a course on Holiness in Biblical Perspective that I taught at Bethel University. In his chapter, Brown critiques

The Humanity of Christ

the reductive physicalism view that human persons are nothing but a body, and that human behavior and personhood can be exhaustively explained simply by means of genetics or neurological cognitive functions of the brain.[1]

In contrast Professor Brown contends that the concept of the human soul arises out of experiences of personal relatedness, and that "personal relatedness designates a realm of unique human capacity and experiences which would include concepts, such as, consciousness of self, personal agency and responsibility, ability to give and receive love, communication with God, and the experience of transcendence."[2] The position adopted in this study is the viewpoint that a critical feature of the biblical portrait of human nature resides in the capacity for *personal relatedness*. Moreover, I agree with Brown's assessment that "the Bible presumes a unique depth and scope of human relatedness that is not assumed for the rest of the animal kingdom."[3] A deduction from this interpretation is that "personal relatedness and the soulful capacities of humans are not the same as [our] cognitive systems or reducible to nothing but cognition." This interpretation further entails that the human experiences of the soul is conditioned by, but "cannot be reduced to the underlying mental process from which they emerge."[4] Professor Brown clarifies, "It is experiences of relatedness to others, to the self, and most particularly to God that endow a person with the attributes that have been [traditionally] attached to the concept of *soul*; that is, experiences of personal relatedness [that] in their depth and complexity create in us that which is semantically designated the soul."[5]

If one accepts Professor Brown's viewpoint that the nature of the human soul constitutes those emergent properties attributed to the experiences of personal relatedness, what, then, fills the vacuum of the generally embraced theological understanding of

1. Brown et al., *Whatever Happened to the Soul*, 100.
2. Ibid.
3. Ibid., 102.
4. Ibid., 103.
5. Ibid., 102.

Setting the Context

the human soul that not only designates that dimension of the self that is immortal and continues beyond death, but also constitutes one of the significant features marking the uniqueness of human persons within the created order of all living things? In other words, with the removal of the interpretation of the human soul as that immortal entity within human nature that persists beyond death, what, then is theologically unique within human nature that constitutes the uniqueness of human persons within the created order of all living things and that simultaneously fulfills this critical substantive gap in the absence of the immortal soul within human nature, and is furthermore not defined as the attributes of emergent properties of brain function? I propose for our reflection that the human spirit is a credible candidate.

Holy Scripture not only speaks of the significance of the human spirit but also of its independent status and distinct role in association with the other constituent features of human nature. For example, consider the Apostle Paul's statement, "Even though I cannot be physically present with you, I will be with you in spirit" (1 Cor 5:3). Or again, consider the text in Hebrews 4:12, in which the human spirit denotes a unique capacity within human nature as an entity associated with but also as independent of the human soul. Hebrews 4:12 states, "For the Word of God is alive and active. Sharper that any double-edged sword; it penetrates even to *dividing soul and spirit*, joints and marrow." Or again, "The grace of the Lord Jesus Christ be with your spirit" (Phil 4:23; Phlm 1:25). Finally, "May your whole spirit, soul, and body be kept blameless" (1 Thess 4:23). Here the Apostle Paul presents the human spirit as a separate entity in addition to but distinct from the body and soul. In addition, it is often said in daily conversation that upon the death of a friend that the physical, concrete body is placed in the grave—now regarded as a corpse, but the spirit of the person ascends to heaven to dwell with God.

If the human spirit is the unique capacity within human nature that enables persons to encounter both God and others, the function of the human spirit, then, has significant implications for living the Christian life.

The Humanity of Christ

It may be helpful at this juncture to note two overarching-undergirding Protestant Evangelical interpretative viewpoints of the Christian life. The difference between the two interpretative perspectives is that of emphasis and focus, but with far-reaching implications for the summons to live a life pleasing to God (1 Thess 4:1, 7). The first viewpoint underscores the basic thesis of the book and expresses the conviction that God created human creatures and redemption in order that through God's love and grace and our continued response to this love and grace we might be restored to our original humanity as created in the image of God. The second interpretive viewpoint, while generally accepted, though often unexamined within a large segment of the Protestant Evangelical Church, can be stated as: God created human creatures in order that they might become Christians.

This second viewpoint implies that the primary purpose of redemption and the work of the Holy Spirit reside exclusively in the task of evangelism; that is, that God views humans as a myriad of individual sinners who need the redemption found in Christ. Clearly, we must never diminish or distort the unalterable biblical teaching that through faith in the redemptive work of Jesus Christ forgiveness of sin is experienced—enabled by the work of the Holy Spirit.

Unfortunately, an inherent problem frequently arises with this perspective when encountering the demands of the Christian life. This problem emerges as the result of a dualistic interpretation of the Christian life. While God does the justifying-forgiving part of the salvation experience, a second demand is inserted; namely, the believer's part. The believer's part entails the responsibility to live holy lives, and to be a faithful and obedient disciple of Christ. Unfortunately, this second part is often understood by believers as a necessary condition for continuing to remain in the grace, love, and blessing of God. If, however, every believer possesses a *sinful nature*, the requirement of the second part becomes not only unrealistic but also impossible. This problem is greatly enhanced if the Christian life is interpreted within a law-based context which is frequently the problem in interpreting the believer's part. Noting

Setting the Context

the fact that the function of the law is to condemn every violation a person commits, as the Apostle Paul states, "The law was brought in so that the trespass might increase" (Rom 5:20), believers having this view are, then, constantly confronted with their limitations and sinfulness regardless of the nature of the offense due to the power of the law. It has been my observation, having served as an interim teaching pastor in over fifteen Protestant Evangelical churches, that many evangelical believers live their Christian life with a large sense of guilt due to the power of the law. Even in the life of a believer who has been renewed by the Spirit, the law exists to condemn every violation, both biblical and those imposed by other sources; such as, denominational ones, etc. This is not meant to imply that the law is evil. But co-opted by sin, the law preforms a duty other than its original purpose. Under the control of the divine Spirit the law becomes a guide for holy living. Klyne Snodgrass argues that the law obtains its function from the sphere in which it is placed; either that of sin or of the Spirit.[6] Nevertheless, in a sin-dominated situation the law brings an intensification of sin even for the believer who has been renewed by the spirit and therefore desires to do the good.

Wolfhart Pannenberg offers insight into this problem in his informative chapter entitled "Protestant Piety and Guilt Consciousness." Pannenberg writes,

> Trust in the promised righteousness outside of us in Christ (extra nos in Christo) presupposes sinfulness as the intrinsic condition of the believer. In a purely forensic conception of justification, believers turn again and again beyond themselves in their concern for the assurance of their salvation, and thus continue to relate themselves to God as sinners.[7]

Pannenberg notes that a split occurs between the extrinsic and the intrinsic aspects of the Christian self, and believers, therefore, experience a failure of a unified self-concept. The conviction, then, unfortunately arises among believers as being basically guilty

---

6. Snodgrass, "Spheres of Influence," 104–5.
7. Pannenberg, *Christian Spirituality*, 20–21.

The Humanity of Christ

sinners before God while seeking to affirm at the same time that they are also as justified-forgiven believers. Unfortunately, the continued emphasis on viewing themselves as sinners emphasizes the need to find assurance of salvation in the face of their failures and sins and that they still belong to God through faith in Christ. This dualism tends to create a feeling of spiritual insecurity toward God and emphasizes the need to prove themselves as worthy recipients of this extraordinary gift of redeeming grace and love. The reassuring biblical text becomes, "For where sin increases, grace increases all the more" (Rom 6:21). The practical implication is that the more believers acknowledge their sinfulness, the more they can be assured that God's saving grace and love is extended toward them.

Ray S. Anderson, with a different purpose, expresses a similar concern:

> Why, despite our preaching on the theme of God's forgiveness through the death of Christ and the atonement of sins completed on the cross, does the power of sin, guilt, and shame seem to have such a stranglehold on those who believe that truth? Sunday after Sunday, many Christians confess their sins and receive absolution, only to live each day with the nagging thought, I pretty well have the idea that he [God] isn't pleased with me! While their confessions have been sincere, the assurance of forgiveness rings hollow. And into this hollowness comes the echo of a bad conscience, accusing and scolding, if not condemning. And so confession becomes a ritual without reality and forgiveness a pronouncement without peace. Again and again we look to the cross in hope of finding that elusive peace, only to come away wounded and weaker.[8]

A theological framework that leaves people lacking in spiritual health and psychological wholeness represents a radical failure to understand the gospel message as good news.[9] Ray Anderson believes that the failure is "because we offer a concept

8. Anderson, *Ministry on the Fireline*, 56.
9. Ibid.

Setting the Context

of forgiveness without the *praxis* of forgiveness and the freedom forgiveness entails."[10] I would add that the failure is also because we understand the gospel message *only* as forgiveness without any concept of freedom that includes hope and restoration. The problem may also be attributed to a neglect of the Holy Spirit's encouraging and strengthening work in the life of believers.

The concern of this book, therefore, includes not only an academic emphasis; that is, to offer a positive interpretation of the nature and function of the human spirit, but also a pastoral one; namely, to recapture the gospel message as not only praxis of forgiveness but also the freedom, and hope, and the restoration of sinners back to function again; that is, to think and to act, according to the virtues that reflect the image of God in which they were originally created.

Upon entering into the redemptive experience of absolute forgiveness through faith in the redemptive work of Jesus Christ, the human spirit is restored back to its foundation and original relationship with the divine Spirit. In this restoration, the Holy Spirit, as the *Agent of Change*, restores the human self dispositionally and motivationally in the core of the human self, creating the desire to serve, worship, honor, and obey God. It is this newly created union with Christ and the newly formed disposition through the indwelling and empowering presence of the divine Spirit that constitutes the source for the emergence of a godly life in the believer through the healing of the human spirit.

This personal-relational capacity within human personhood was functionally inaugurated with the creation of the woman Eve. The creation of the woman constitutes an essential component in God's vision and purpose of an I-Thou communal relational experience within humanity. In short, God created humans to be *persons-in-community*. This interpretation begins with the biblical statement, "The Lord God said, 'It is not good for the man to be alone, I will make a helper suitable for him'" (Gen 2:18). (I interpret the word *helper* as a compatible and supportive companion.) The biblical account continues, God brought the living creatures

10. Ibid.

The Humanity of Christ

and presented them to *man* (Adam) to see what he would name them (Gen 2:19–20). "So the man gave names to all the livestock, the birds in the sky, and all the wild animals. But for Adam no suitable helper was found" (Gen 2:20). The naming of the animals is not an isolated or insignificant incident. Adam looked deep within the created order to find a counterpart that would complete and complement his unique relational capacity. It is only with the creation of the woman that a relational encounter or meeting is made possible that manifests a remarkable unity within diversity that mirrors the interactive communion within the Trinitarian nature of God. This relational capacity, moreover, constitutes the uniqueness of human persons as created in the image of God. This relational capacity has its creaturely ground in the human spirit and its foundational ground in relationship with the Divine Spirit.

I acknowledge at the outset that proposing an interpretation of the precise nature and function of the human spirit in relation to the divine Spirit and its implication for the spiritual development of the life of believers is a demanding task. To introduce this task, I will begin with the excellent study of John Welker in his book *God the Spirit*.

Welker's study is important since he offers an interpretation of God as Spirit that he believes advances beyond "the traditional interpretations that he designates as the old European metaphysis and the Western theological-pietistic thought forms which include social moralism that he believes limits the Spirit's power to heal and [spiritually] revive [restore] humans."[11] Welker's view is presented because of his defining focus, though specifically applied to God, offers insights into the nature and function of the divine Spirit, specifically the Spirit's power to create community.

Welker's stated approach, however, is a postmodern one, a perspective he believes "affords the sensibilities to connect pluralism and individualism in a manner that retains the values of both because this approach is sensitive to the differences and builds on assumptions of a reality or realities that consist of a reality of

---

11. Welker, *God the Spirit*, 41–43.

Setting the Context

structural patterns of life and of the interconnectedness with each other."[12]

The function of the Spirit, states Welker, "is to create community that entails placing persons in a conscious solidarity of responsibility and love." In this Spirit-created community, writes Welker,

> Persons can accept their own finitude and perishability, [and] can live with the clear consciousness of the perishability of their relative world because they know that in and beyond this perishability, they are ordained to participate in the divine glory. Persons in the community of the Spirit are aware of their public significance and worth in view of the significance and worth of their fellow creatures, and in view of God's glorification. As participants in this community affected by the Spirit, people change themselves, each other, and the world by free self-withdrawal for the benefit of their fellow creatures. With free self-withdrawal for the benefit of others, they become a domain of power in the Spirit of shared participation.[13]

To explain the unifying power of the divine Spirit, Welker adopts the metaphor of a force field that unites person in a community of equality that stands in contrast to the perception of the spirit in the Western world.[14] Welker, however, does not want to attribute the notion of person to the Holy Spirit as in Western theology, especially if the notion of spirit is understood by analogy with an individual center of action or as a being in-and-for itself alone; that is, "as one ego beside other egos,"[15] "standing over against others and affecting self-differentiation in relation to them."[16] At the same time, however, he does not reject completely the notion of person as applicable to the Holy Spirit. Rather than interpreting the spirit as an independent center of willing consciousness,

12. Ibid., 37–38.
13. Ibid., 282.
14. Ibid., 238.
15. Ibid.
16. Ibid., 281.

The Humanity of Christ

Welker views the Holy Spirit as *public person*.[17] By public person he interprets the personhood of the Spirit in terms of concrete manifestations of complete selflessness that finds its specific revelation in the person of Jesus Christ.[18]

To clarify more fully the Spirit as public person, Welker introduces the phrase a *web of formative relationships*. This phrase is, then, further connected with the phrase *domain of resonance*, which entails a centered multiplicity of relations of resonance, meaning formative relationships. Welker writes,

> A person acquires the features of personhood only by being formed in diverse webs of relationships . . . As persons, we are complex composites such as we are children of our parents, a relative of our relatives, friends, colleagues of our colleagues, contemporaries of our contemporaries.[19]

We are not persons because we have independent centers of consciousness but because we stand in webs of resonance (formative relationships) that help to shape us as much as we help to shape them. As the public domain of resonance, the person of the Spirit of God simply denotes the power of God's presence that transforms, empowers, and liberates from the power of sin that distorts and disintegrates genuine community resonance.

If I understand Welker correctly, the Spirit is the powerful presence of God that transforms persons so that they see and interact with others as God intended humans to view and embrace others with the result of forming a community of the Spirit. The mystery and power of the self-giving presence of the Spirit of self-withdrawal from the egotistic spirit of the world, is revealed and inaugurated in persons filled with the Spirit. Persons in communion with the Holy Spirit not only grasp the mystery of sacrifice and the freedom of free self-withdrawal but also become witnesses of the

---

17. Ibid., 312.
18. Ibid.
19. Ibid., 313.

Setting the Context

life-giving Spirit.[20] Persons or communities filled with the Spirit of Christ, therefore, are "in the Spirit of love, of righteousness and of peace" and "work against the power of the spirit of self-interest, self-promotion, injustice, and egoism that seeks to isolate [and] separate people, and confine them to solitary and disintegrated communities."[21]

Before undertaking the task of clarifying the nature and function of the human spirit, it would be helpful to set forth several contextual presuppositions that undergird the proposed thesis of the relational significance of the human spirit as the essence of human personhood. I am designating these presuppositions as contextual because of their contributing or supporting role. While not specifically developed within the body of the book, they nevertheless are essential concepts that clarify and support the basic thesis of the book.

CONTRIBUTING PRINCIPLES

Undergirding the premise of the book that the uniqueness of human persons resides in the possession of the human spirit expressed in the formation of community is clarified by several contextual principles or presuppositions.

Principle One

The biblical concept of the human soul simply denotes the life-substance of human existence. Hence, the soul refers to the breath of life that endues the physical and neurological functions of the body. Apart from this breath of life the human person would cease to exist. While Holy Scripture uses different terms to convey the soulish dimensions of human existence, the primary biblical term comes from the creation narrative of the Old Testament; namely, *nephesh*. The New Testament writers, on the other hand, selected

20. Ibid., 310.
21. Ibid., 282.

The Humanity of Christ

the word *psyche* to interpret nephesh. Unfortunately the word psyche carries philosophical implications from the use of the Greek language that has contributed to a dualistic understanding of human nature. The word psyche has also come to denote in much of Western theological thought and specifically in the development of the discipline of psychology to denote the inner or spiritual-intellectual psychological dimension of human nature, which is often accorded greater value and significance in contrast with the physical-external dimensions of human nature.

One fact, however, remains unequivocally true; as humans, we are creaturely, biologically conditioned beings. Ray S. Anderson defines creatureliness as "the broad continuum of organism inhabiting the natural world and carrying that indefinable, but absolutely necessary, breath of life."[22] Anderson further clarifies, "The creaturely is of creation, bound up in the solidarity of life which is from the earth and dependent on its environment for the relative span of time allotted to it."[23] Humans, therefore, along with the nonhuman creatures, are bound together by the possession of the breath of life as a gift of the life-giving Spirit of God. "It is life," writes Anderson, "suspended in time by the fragile mystery that binds breath to flesh and connects nerve to muscle."[24]

Two biblical facts reinforce the use of the word nephesh as conveying the meaning—the breath of life. The first fact is the recognition that the word nephesh is applied to nonhuman creatures in the biblical creation narrative denoting the possession of the breath of life—translated into English as living beings. Hence, humans possess a commonality with all creatures that possess the breath of life. Paul Jewett's comments reinforce this way of understanding the word nephesh.

> It is better . . . to think of the soul in personal categories. While there is an ineluctable relationship between soul and body, the soul is not some spiritual substance "in" the body as a fetus is "in" the womb. Nor is it a spiritual

22. Anderson, *On Being Human*, 20.
23. Ibid.
24. Ibid.

Setting the Context

substance diffused through the body as blood "through" the veins. Rather, the soul is just the personal self, the "I," animating the body and manifest in a bodily way.²⁵

The soul, therefore, is simply the life of the body and, therefore, not an independent acting agent as such. On the other hand, as the life of the body, the soul emits properties that characterize and support a living and active creature. While maintaining the premise that creatureliness is an essential component of being human, creatureliness does not contain in its powers the purpose for which humanity is called into being.

Wolfhart Pannenberg adds to our reflections,

> The soul (nephesh) is not another component part of a human being over and above the body, as in Cartesian or Platonic dualism. It is simply the bodily being as living . . . But insofar as the soul is the life of its body, it is an effect of the life giving spirit. The divine creative spirit causes human beings to have life within them, and to that extent the spirit is internally present to them, although it does not on that account become a "part" of them.²⁶

To conclude: the thesis is proposed that the absolute distinguishing component of human nature that differentiates humans from nonhuman creatures is the possession of the human spirit. The human spirit is the capacity inherent within human creatureliness that enables humans to engage in personal relatedness that in complexity and depth of encounter differentiates humans from the nonhuman creatures. It is a gift of God that enables the humans to function beyond the deterministic cycles of creation to which all other creatures are bound, enabling humans to enter into personal fellowship with God without, at the same time, breaking the bond of solidarity shared with all other creaturely beings that possess the breath of life. It is the argument of this study, then, that it is the possession of the human spirit that marks human creatures as unique within the order of creaturely beings.

---

25. Jewett and Shuster, *Who We Are*, 42.
26. Pannenberg, *Anthropology in Theological Perspective*, 523.

The Humanity of Christ

Some may argue, however, that the notion of spirit is applied to the nonhuman creatures in the biblical record. Here the biblical text recorded in Ecclesiastes 3:11 is central to the argument. The text reads, "Who knows if the spirit of man rises upward and if the spirit of the animal goes down into the earth?" Here the word *spirit* is applied both to humans and to nonhuman creatures. The context of this biblical text, however, is critical. The context of the biblical passage focuses on the notion of set times and their power over us all. The author asserts that a time is set for humanity to learn the truth about human life and its actions. The thrust is that "humankind is on a journey from dust to dust, with the irony that we die like cattle [though] we fancy ourselves as gods."[27]

The author of Ecclesiastes writes, "As for men God tests them [humans] so that they may see that they are like the animals" (3:18). Verse 17 reinforces the thought, focusing upon "life" reversals and sudden shifts . . . "For if anything cries out to be reversed, it is injustice."[28] "I said in my heart," declares the author, "God will judge the righteous and the wicked, for he has appointed a time for every matter, and for every work" (Eccl 3:17).

The question, then, arises whether anything within us survives death? The author replied, "Who knows?" That is, "if the spirit of man rises upward and if the spirit of the animal goes down to the earth" (3:11). Derek Kidner proposes a commendable interpretation of the use of spirit in Ecclesiastes:

> Breath or Spirit, in these verses, is the life God gives to animals and men alike, whose withdrawal means their death . . . Clearly we have at least that much in common with the beasts; but whether spirit implies anything eternal in us, no-one can decide by observation.[29] . . . From an observation of daily life, the author is simply stating nothing more than the fact that God gives and withdraws the life-breath at will.[30]

---

27. Kidner, *Message of Ecclesiastes*, 42.
28. Ibid.
29. Ibid.
30. Ibid., 43.

Setting the Context

Whether the use of spirit implies anything immortal in us is not the focus of the author and therefore does not stand in contradiction to the proposed assertion that the uniqueness of humans lies in the possession of spirit. In this context, spirit becomes synonymous with the soul or the life of all creatures and conveys nothing more than the fact that humans, along with animals, possess the gift of life, and from natural observations nothing more can be said.

If someone would choose to apply the notion of spirit to both animals and humans, Karl Barth offers an insightful interpretation. Barth asserts that spirit is not something which the person is, in the sense that a person is both body and soul. Rather, a person has spirit or, to put it another way, *spirit has him*.[31] Spirit does not belong to humans by virtue of creaturely being, such as soul and body, rather spirit belongs to God and it is given to humans as an endowment. In the broadest sense, spirit simply denotes the interaction of God on his creatures.

Neither soul nor spirit, therefore, contends Karl Barth, can be denied to nonhuman creatures. The distinction is that the nonhuman soul has a spiritual determination that extends only to its natural existence as a creature created by the Creator.[32] The human person, on the other hand, has a double determination in which humans are determined in the same way as nonhuman creatures to be creaturely beings, but in that determination is also determined to respond to God's Word and to share God's destiny of immortal existence. Here Barth, notes Ray Anderson, "inserts a radical principle of grace in his theological anthropology" that I find compelling.[33] Since the human spirit is a gift from God, contends Barth, "the distinction between humans and the nonhuman can be made only as a theological postulate, and not as an inference drawn from any phenomenological analysis."[34]

---

31. Barth, *Doctrine of Creation*, 354ff.
32. Ibid., 354.
33. Anderson, *On Being Human*, 211.
34. Barth, *Doctrine of Creation*, 361.

The Humanity of Christ

Principle Two

When encountering the findings or studies from the human sciences, I adopt an Christological hermeneutic. This hermeneutical approach differs from that of, for example, Wolfhart Pannenberg, as expressed in his book, *Anthropology in Theological Perspective*. Pannenberg begins his studies by asking if Christian theology can reasonably claim universal validity in our contemporary world. His answer is a qualified yes, but only if theological claims are supported by the objective, scientific studies of human nature. Pannenberg's approach entails the provisional acceptance of the secular description of human nature, which in turn, he contends, can be expanded and clarified as a result of showing that the secular descriptions of human nature, may in fact, contain theologically relevant dimensions. To support and confirm Pannenberg's fundamental theology by objective studies of humanity from the data of the natural sciences and secondarily reinforced by theological insight, I believe, diminishes the significance of theological reflection and its contribution for understanding human nature, I find unacceptable.[35]

I find agreement with James Loder's methodological approach, and also that of Thomas G. Weinandy in his book *In the Likeness of Sinful Flesh*,[36] in which the formation of a theological understanding of what it means to be human lies in God's self-revelation in the person of Jesus Christ. I further propose that the material substance of God's self-revelation in the humanity of Jesus Christ guides and instructs my methodological approach. Hence, I concur with James Loder who adopts the Chalcedonian model as a way of working both methodologically and materially from below and above at the same time, "allowing the objective of revelation to deal transformatively with the objectivity of the natural sciences."[37]

---

35. Loder, *Logic of the Spirit*, 28.
36. Weinandy, *In the Likeness of Sinful Flesh*, 17–19.
37. Loder, *Logic of the Spirit*, 195.

Setting the Context

Principle Three

The first human creatures were created ontologically or essentially good; that is, there was originally no dualistic tension within the nature of our ancient ancestors between good and evil. Theologian Dale Moody concurs,

> According to the biblical view, creation may become corrupt, but it is not in itself evil. When it is corrupt, it is a good thing spoiled. God's intention in all creation is to manifest his glory in his manifold goodness. And deviation from this good intention is natural evil . . . and sin when it involves the will of man.[38]

Hence, a fundamental undergirding presupposition is the contention that humans were originally created ontologically good, but became existentially estranged from God as a result of their disobedience; that is, their idolatrous displacement of God and failure to trust in God's command. Humanity's original righteousness or goodness justitia originalis became distorted through original sin, reversing the original positive relation with God to a negative expression in which the human self stands over against God and others as an autonomous self, motivated by self-interest. Moreover, the human spirit has become dysfunctional in its spiritual discernment of the truth of God. The Apostle Paul writes, "The person without the Spirit does not accept the things that come from the Spirit of God but consider them foolishness, and cannot understand them because they are discerned only through the Spirit" (1 Cor 2:14).

Principle Four

God originally designed reality to be communal and hence relational. The undergirding presupposition is that God cannot create a solitary being and declare that being to be in the image of God. Gregory of Nazianzus, for example, asserted that the inner life of

---

38. Moody, *Word of Truth*, 145.

The Humanity of Christ

the Trinity is relational.[39] James Loder agrees, stating that for human nature to partake in the divine Spirit is to participate in the inner life of God.[40] It is this relational dynamic fundamental within the Christian worldview that differentiates the Christian concept of reality from most, if not all, other views of reality.[41]

This interactive relational component and the transformational power of the human spirit can be viewed from the studies of what James Loder designates as the Interactionist psychological approach. This approach is helpful in that it operates from the premise the reality is fundamentally relational and connects this relational core with the human spirit. Consider, for example, the work of Sigmund Freud as noted by James Loder as an illustration of this point. What Freud found in the unconscious life through dream analysis and free association techniques—his path to the unconscious, states James Loder, is a dual drive theory of motivation; namely, a life instinct (eros, pleasure) and a death instinct.[42]

Believing that an interaction existed between the conscious and the unconscious life, Freud viewed the emergence of the life/death instinct as performing a fundamental role in the creation of a sense of ultimacy that he regarded as a manifestation of the human spirit.[43] To suggest that the human spirit is the interactive force between the conscious and unconscious life, I believe to be an insightful notion.

The belief that relationality or interaction between consciousness and unconsciousness is central to comprehending reality and that the ground and the source of this relational interaction is the human spirit, I find compelling. As humans, we experience the spirit as the interpretative ground through which all things find their true identity in relationship. Amos Yong concurs, "It is the

---

39. Nazianzus, *Logic of the Spirit*, 195.
40. Loder and Neidhardt, *Knight's Move*, 293–94.
41. Pringle-Pattison, *Idea of God in the Light of Recent Philosophy*, 291.
42. Loder, *Logic of the Spirit*, 21.
43. Ibid.

Setting the Context

human spirit that illuminates the symbolic structure of reality that enables us both to know and to develop as human persons."[44]

The conviction, therefore, is advanced that the sustaining and transformational dynamic in human personhood lies in the capacity of the human spirit. This presupposition will be developed more fully at a later point. Acknowledging the transformational dynamic of the human spirit, it is proposed that the human spirit functions as the executive director of soul, or life of each person, guiding our relational encounters. The conviction is furthermore advanced that this transformational dynamic of the human spirit has its true function and home only when it is in one accord with the divine Spirit.

Lesslie Newbigin advances our understanding of the relational dynamic of human existence as it relates to the creation of humans and the purpose of salvation. Newbigin writes,

> Human life from its beginning is a life of shared relationship in the context of a task—a task that is continuous with God's creative work in the natural world. In contrast to those forms of spirituality that seek the real self by looking within, the Bible invites us to see the real human life as a life of shared relationships in a world of living creatures and created things, a life of mutual personal responsibility for the created world, its animal and vegetable life and its resources of soil and water and air. This, and no other, is the real human life, which is the object of God's primal blessing and of his saving purpose . . . In short, the Bible invites us to see the really human, but not by looking within and finding at the core of human reality a purely spiritual entity that is the object of God's saving purpose. On the contrary, the [Bible] invites us to see the really human as the life of mutual responsibility for the created world and therefore to see God's saving purpose in terms of this real world of real people.[45]

Newbigin continues,

---

44. Yong, *Discerning the Spirit(s)*, 131.
45. Newbigin, *Open Secret*, 69–70.

The Humanity of Christ

This is because God is no solitary [being]. The unreal picture of human beings as isolated spiritual monads; that is, an indestructible unit; a single and indivisible substance, belongs to the same world of thought as the picture of God as an isolated spiritual [being]. The reality is not so; God, as revealed to us in the gospel, is not an [isolated being]. Interpersonal relatedness belongs to the very being of God. Therefore there can be no salvation for human beings except in relatedness. No one can be made whole except by being restored to the wholeness of that being-in-relatedness for which God made us . . . and that is the image of that being-in-relatedness which is the being of God himself.[46]

Baruch A. Levine contributes to this understanding when he writes,

The biblical God is a god of community . . . God's purpose could not be realized through royal dynasties and chosen leader, or through personal covenants. The covenants with the Patriarchs and the dynasty covenants with the House of David are based on the concept that fulfillment of the promise depends on the character of collective life, not on the virtues of illustrious individuals . . . The idea of chosenness, with its emphasis on the holy as a goal of collective existence, took up the slack created by notions of transcendence . . . The historic experience of the Israelite people was ultimately meant to serve as a model for all nations . . . This relationship allowed the Israelites to approach [their] transcendent God more intimately than one would have expected.[47]

Principle Five

The biblical concept of *reality* is, first and foremost, *communal* and *restorative*, not exclusively *forensic*, though the forensic elements are not to be diminished by the communal and restorative thrust

46. Ibid., 70.
47. Levine, "Language of Holiness," 254.

Setting the Context

of the biblical message. This presupposition entails the premise that salvation is more than forgiveness, though the forgiveness-justification dimension of salvation is indispensable, but centers on the restoration both of humans and creation so that they may again express God's ultimate purpose in creating them. God's ultimate purpose in redemption is that creation and humanity will be made *whole* again according to the purpose for which God originally created them.

Veli-Matti Karkkainen makes a similar point when he writes,

> The saving act of the righteous and just God is not only about the salvation of individuals by faith such as that exhibited by Abraham (Rom 4), but harks back to the very beginnings and whole of history of humankind. The redemption God accomplished through the life, death, and resurrection of Christ in God's divine Purpose, aims at the restoration of the whole creation (Rom 8:22).[48]

I find Professor Karkkainen's interpretation of justification and restoration is similar to my own. While justification is foundational for God's granting forgiveness of sin, I would suggest that justification is the foundation upon which God's righteousness in Christ for salvation is imputed to sinners but also makes possible the gift of the Holy Spirit infused into the life of every believer that enables sinners to participate in the fellowship and life of God.

On the basis of Christ's redemptive work, the Holy Spirit, as the divine *Agent of Change*, cancels our estrangement from God, and our sin, guilt and death entrenched in our humanity via a transforming relation between the divine and human natures within the incarnate reality of Jesus Christ. Hence, the "incarnation is inherently redemptive and redemption is intrinsically incarnational."[49]

As the divine Agent of Change, the Holy Spirit enables the human spirit to submit to God's declaration that we are indeed sinners needing forgiveness and simultaneously initiates the hope of the ultimate restoration of both believers and creation in God's

---

48. Karkkainen, in Beilby and Eddy, eds., *Justification: Five Views*, 239.
49. T. F. Torrance, *The Trinitarian Faith*, 65.

The Humanity of Christ

final restoration of all things. I, therefore, agree with Professor Karkkainen's statement; namely, "that justification and theosis is not in principle a problematic synthesis."[50]

My earlier assertion is now hopefully clearer; namely, that God calls us to be Christians in order that through divine grace and our continued response to divine grace we might become fully human according to the image of God in which we were originally created. While God's grace in justification restores a *sonship* relationship with God, it also entails the promise of the ultimate restoration of our humanity as well that of creation itself.

Principle Six

The human spirit has become *dysfunctional* and distorted due to its loss of relationship with God and the entrance of sin into human existence. The divine judgment for sin upon humanity, writes the Apostle Paul, is expressed in the phrase God *gave them over* (Rom 1:24, 26, 28). The phrase *gave them over*, I interpret as God's withdrawal of the demands of his guiding and protective Word, allowing other lords and powers to take control. In other words, the judgment for sin was sin itself, allowing sin to prevail over the created order. Paul Achtemeier interprets the phrase *God gave them over* in the context and meaning of the Wrath of God this way:

> The wrath of God, in sum, consists in letting humanity carry out the results of its idolatrous rejection of the Creator as Lord. That our present world and our own society is beginning to resemble ever more closely what Paul describes in verse 24–28 [and] should therefore be seen in this perspective. Freedom for us to do what we want is the punishment of our rebellion against God. A celebration of life freed from the constraints of the Word of God is therefore a celebration of the visitation of God's wrath upon humankind.[51]

---

50. Ibid., 239.
51. Achtemeier, *Romans*, 40.

Setting the Context

The consequence of humanity's idolatrous rejection of the Creator's guiding Word resulted not only in separation from fellowship with God but also the dysfunction of the human spirit. It is, furthermore, proposed that the dysfunction of the human spirit centers not only in the reversal of its originally designed purpose to love, trust, and honor God and to love one's neighbor as one's self, but also upon the entrance of death into creaturely existence with all its decaying and distorting effects (Rom 5:12).[52] The phrase *dysfunction of the human spirit*, therefore, is used here as a synonym for the traditional phrase *sinful nature*. Consider the many biblical texts that state the consequence of death as the result of the entrance of sin into the world. A key biblical text, for example, is: "For the wages of sin is death" (Rom 3:23).

An alternative interpretation of original sin that has dominated the Western Christian church since Augustine teaches that inherited guilt and corruption has been imputed to all humankind as a consequence of Adam's original sin. Briefly stated, this interpretation of Rom 5:12b, following the exegesis of Augustine, translated into Latin as *quo omnes peccaverunt*, and translated in our English Bibles as *because all have sinned*. The interpretation of inherited guilt and corruption places specific emphasis on the phrase ἐφ' ᾧ παντα ἥρμαρτον ("in whom all have sinned") in which ἐφ' ᾧ is translated as ("because") is applied to the verb, sinned, and is furthermore applied to the pronoun *all*. Through the influence of Augustine, this phrase in Romans 5:12b came to mean that *all persons have sinned*, applying the *because* to mean that sin was imputed to all persons due to seminal union with Adam. Hence, the deduction from the text was that all humans were numerically in Adam so that when Adam sinned, all persons were constituted as guilty, condemned sinners as the result of Adam's act of disobedience. This interpretation continues to be used by the Western church to teach the doctrine of inherited guilt and corruption from Adam's disobedience and that the judgment of sin and its corruption was imputed to all of Adam's descendants.

---

52. Meyendorff, *Byzantine Theology*, 144.

The Humanity of Christ

An alternative interpretation was developed by the Greek Patristic Fathers. They translated Romans 5:12b to read, "Therefore just as sin entered the world through one man, and death through sin, in this way death came to all people, because of death all persons are constituted as sinners."[53] The Greek Patristic tradition maintained that the judgment of sin was death and was taught by Greek Patristic Fathers such as Theodore of Mopsuestia, Theodoret of Cyrus, Gregory Palamas, and the highly regarded Maximus the Confessor. Maximus taught that persons were personally responsible for their own acts of sin and did not incur inherited corruption and imputed guilt from Adam's disobedience. He furthermore believed that the consequence of Adam's sin resides with the mind's submission to the flesh. He also asserted that inherited guilt and corruption advocated by the Western teachers constituted an inaccurate interpretation of Romans 5:12. Maximus and the other leaders maintained that the consequence of the original sin committed by Adam ignited human passions and imposed morality and death on all humankind. John Chryssavgis summarizes the Orthodox viewpoint when he writes,

> Death and corruption, understood in a personalized sense, has in this way been viewed in the east as a cosmic, tyrannical disease that holds humanity and the whole of creation under its sway, both spiritually and physically. Mortality is the "murderer from the beginning" (Jn 8:44). It is through death that sin is seen to exercise its power. According to the Greek Fathers death renders sin inevitable because one struggles in order to survive . . . The imminent threat of death forces us to sin in order to retain our existence.[54]

This Byzantine theological viewpoint, then, did not center on overcoming the imputed corruption and guilt imposed by Adam's disobedience, a concern that even today dominates Western Christianty, but rather focuses on the hope and joy of participating in the life of God. Hence the Eastern Greek branch of the Christian

---

53. Ibid.
54. Ormerod, *Grace and Disgrace*, 198–199.

Setting the Context

faith, in my opinion, held a more positive or hopeful outlook on the Christian life as opposed to a more *negative* sinful interpretation stressed by the Western Christian church;[55] that is, a dominating, law-oriented concentration on personal sinfulness with a goal of establishing assurance that God's forgiving grace toward us as sinners still abounds (Rom 6:20). The Eastern Greek Church, then, initiated a more *positive* outlook in terms of the Christian pursuit of participation in the life of God. I do not interpret *participation* in the life of God as the divinization of the believer. Rather, I concur with T. F. Torrance that

> *theosis* or *theopoiesis* is not the divining or deification of the human soul or creaturely being, but rather is the Spirit of God's humanizing and personalizing us by uniting us with Christ's vicarious humanity in a way that both confirms us in our creaturely reality utterly different from God and yet also adapts us in our contingent nature or knowledge of God for communion with God and for fellowship with one another.[56]

Principle Seven

The restoration of creation and specifically that of humanity resides not only in the life, death, and resurrection of Christ but also, and in a theologically significant way, in the incarnation of Christ. Through the incarnation, Jesus sanctifies human nature, making possible through union with him the *first fruits* of the restoration of human personhood. The premise underlying this conviction is that Jesus Christ is the only truly human person that has ever existed in the world. Christ took our place, faced every temptation, and overcame the dictatorial power of sin and death for the sake of humankind. Hence, Jesus became the *vicarious human* for our sakes. The humanity of Christ, therefore, constitutes an essential dimension in the defeat of the power of sin and death and the

---

55. Ibid., 145.
56. Colyer, *How to Read T. F. Torrance*, 179.

The Humanity of Christ

restoration of humanity. Thomas G. Weinandy makes the same point when he writes,

> Jesus' human nature is absolutely essential if we are to comprehend clearly what Jesus accomplished, in and though his humanity, on the cross, and in his resurrection. Ultimately, our salvation is unconditionally dependent upon the Son's assuming a humanity disfigured by sin and freely acting as a son of Adam.[57]

The importance and significance of the incarnation for the restoration of human persons finds expression in the thought of T. F. Torrance and is faithfully summarized by Elmer M. Colyer:

> In the hypostatic union, the Son of God assumed our [distorted and rebellious] humanity in conflict with God. This does not mean that Jesus Christ the incarnate Son sinned himself or became contaminated by our corrupt and fallen condition. Rather it signifies that the hypostatic union is a reconciling union in which the Son of God condemned sin in our sinful humanity and overcame the estrangement, sin, guilt and death entrenched in our humanity via a transforming relation between the divine and human natures within the incarnate reality of Jesus Christ . . . The incarnation, therefore, is inherently redemptive and redemption is intrinsically incarnational.[58]

T. F. Torrance clarifies this interpretation in his book *The Meditation of Christ*,

> In the Incarnation Christ has penetrated the dark depths and alienation from God, [by] taking our fallen and diseased humanity on himself in order to get at the very ontological roots of sin and guilt entrenched in the recesses of human existence.[59]

An *Atoning Exchange* occurred in which Christ in his self-abnegating and sacrificial love took our place that we might have

---

57. Weinandy, *In the Likeness of Sinful Flesh*, 18–19.
58. Colyer, *How to Read T. F. Torrance*, 85.
59. Torrance, *Trinitarian Faith*, 65.

Setting the Context

his place, becoming what we are that we might become what he is. The Apostle Paul writes, "God made him who had no sin *to be sin for us*, so that in him we might become the righteousness of God" (2 Cor 2:21). And again in the Epistle to the Hebrews the author writes, "Since the children have flesh and blood, he too shared in their humanity so that by his death he might break the power of him who holds the power of death—that is, the devil—and free those who all their lives were held in slavery by their fear of death" (Heb 4:14–15).

The significance of the incarnation and the freedom Christ purchased for us by his life, death, and resurrection also includes the incarnation that means that God himself came in Jesus Christ to save us in "the heart of our fallen and depraved humanity, where humanity is at its wickedest in its enmity and violence against the reconciling love of Christ."[60]

Karl Barth expressed and summarized the significance of Jesus' *becoming human* in the context of Christ's admonition to love one's neighbor as one's self:

> The neighbor becomes real humanity through the incarnation. No new ethical criterion has been introduced through the humanity of Jesus. The original and basic form of human as fellow humanity has been renewed and brought under the saving determination of God. The neighbor is not first of all an ethical construct based on some general ethical principle of duty or even of love. The neighbor is both God and the other. To deny the other as neighbor is to deny God. To recognize the other as neighbor is to recognize the good and the right as the demand of God on men through [his/her] neighbor.[61]

To conclude: The restoration of the human spirit through union with the divine Spirit constitutes the foundation for a realistic expectation of the divine promise of *new life*; that is, a renewed way of thinking and acting on the basis of Christ's life, death, and resurrection. This also entails an extraordinary experience of the

---

60. Torrance, *Mediation of Christ*, 39.
61. Barth, *Humanity of God*, 46.

The Humanity of Christ

love and grace in which Christ as a *vicarious human* unites us with God who through the hypostatic union in which Christ heals our lost and distorted human existence, so that we might become sharers in the triune life of God (2 Pet 1:3–4).

2

The Nature and Function of the Human Spirit

For the Spirit searches everything, even the depths of God. For what human being knows what is truly human except the human spirit that is within?

—1 Cor 2:10b–11

INTRODUCING THE THESIS

THE DIVINELY CREATED PURPOSE of the human spirit is no longer consistently visible within the human community since the human spirit is existentially estranged from its essential foundation in God and by association with the divine Spirit. Hence, the only definitive, visible manifestation of a genuine expression of the human spirit as God intended is revealed to us in Jesus Christ. James Loder writes,

> In Jesus Christ's nature as fully divine and fully human, we have the model of personal relatedness through which

The Humanity of Christ

all our expressions of personal and social relatedness can be assessed.[1]

As the *executive director* of the soul, the life of the person, the human spirit is that dimension of human nature that enables persons to act and to react toward others in a manner that mirrors the spiritual and moral character of God. To reflect theologically on this proposed thesis, several scholars have been conscripted who discuss in varying degrees the significance of the human spirit. These teachers are Soren Kierkegaard, Wolfhart Pannenberg, Karl Barth, T. F. Torrance, Ray S. Anderson, George Hendry, James E. Loder, and Warren S. Brown. While some of these scholars write more directly about the human spirit and its association with the divine Spirit, all offer insight into the nature and function of the human spirit and its compatibility with the divine Spirit. The specific goal here centers on introducing those various concepts that will assist us in clarifying the nature and function of the human spirit and the necessity of the healing of the human spirit through restored relationship with God (who is Spirit), so that the human spirit may begin again to function according to the pattern of *imago Dei* revealed in the person of Jesus Christ.

PHILOSOPHICAL-THEOLOGICAL REFLECTIONS

(1) *James E. Loder*:

"Spirit refers to a *quality of relationality*; it is a way to conceptualize the dynamic interactive unity by which two disparate things are held together without loss of their diversity."[2] "The human spirit," writes Loder, "makes all acts of human intelligence self-transcendent and self-relational."[3]

(2) *Soren Kierkegaard*:

The human being is spirit. But what is spirit? Spirit is the self. But what is the self? The self is a relation that relates

---

1. Loder and Neidhardt, *Knight's Move*, 10.
2. Loder and Neidhardt, *Knight's Move*, 10.
3. Ibid., 12.

The Nature and Function of the Human Spirit

to itself or is the relation's relating itself to itself in the relation; the self is not the relation but is the relation's relating itself to itself.[4]

(3) *Donald L. Alexander*:

The human spirit refers to an orientation, an openness to the world, an *exocentric centeredness* or capacity that, while not divorced from our biologically conditioned life, nevertheless in depth and complexity reaches beyond it in encounters of personal relatedness. *To reach beyond* is intended to convey a personal capacity for self-transcendence; that is, to reach (go) beyond the given-ness of the natural in the instinctual equipment of human creatureliness and their relations to their biological capacities, or to transcend the immediacy of the present, described as human *openness* to the world and to the future. In the New Testament the human spirit is often associated with synonyms, such as the *heart* and the *mind*. I propose, however, that the human spirit is the conscious substratum of all our mental acts and interacts with the body and its physical states and their properties in such a way that it determines the brain-states which are the correlates to the beliefs and desires which make up the structure of the soul.

(4) *Robert M. Torrance*:

As the animal most imperfectly programmed by nature for the period between life and death, the animal that must seek to acquire what it characteristically lacks to begin with, and to actualize by directed effort what is potential in its being but never knowable in advance, the human species may be designated *animal quarenens* [questing animal] with at least as much right as *animal rationale* [rational animal], . . . only if we view it as seeking for something beyond its reach, it achieves awareness, and hence can be fully a *quest*, first in man; and not until man posits a mobile dimension at least partly independent of biological need does the quest become

---

4. Kierkegaard, *Sickness unto Death*, 13.

The Humanity of Christ

spiritual and specially human. It lies in the nature of *spirit*.[5]

CHARACTERISTICS OF THE HUMAN SPIRIT

Kierkegaard: The Spiritual Self as a Relational Self

In an opaque passage in his book *Sickness unto Death*, Soren Kierkegaard designates the human person as essentially *spirit*. As quoted above, Kierkegaard writes,

> The human being is spirit. But what is spirit? Spirit is the self. But what is the self? The self is a relation that relates to itself or is the relation's relating itself to itself in the relation; the self is not the relation but is the relation's relating itself to itself.

In this complex passage Kierkegaard views the human person as *spirit*, which is the human dimension that embodies the capacity for self-relational encounters. This self-relational capacity constitutes an essential component of being a human person. The human person, therefore, is not understood simply as an entity independent of relationality; that is, as an isolate being. Rather, the human person by constitution is a relational being right down to the core of human personhood.[6] As a spiritual self, the human person actualizes itself in and through its relational capacity, enabling reflection upon itself both as a subject as well as an object of its own self-reflective thought.

The human self as spirit, however, is not simply a self-interacting being. This self-relational capacity also constitutes the ontological ground for relational interaction outside oneself; that is, with others. Kierkegaard writes, "The human self is . . . a relation that relates itself to itself and in relating itself to itself relates itself to another."[7] In a different, yet complementary, context, the

---

5. Torrance, *Spiritual Quest*, 3–4.
6. Evans, *Soren Kierkegaard's Christian Psychology*, 46.
7. Kierkegaard, *Sickness unto Death*, 13.

The Nature and Function of the Human Spirit

Chinese philosopher, Confucius, makes a similar observation, "A person cannot be *humane* [virtuous] apart from his/her neighbor."[8] In other words, the human person cannot be understood fully in isolation or a lack of interaction with others since the individual self is not a simple entity but entails a complex capacity for relationship between two disparate things. James Loder expresses a complementary understanding of the human spirit when he writes "The human spirit is a quality of relationality; it is a way to conceptualize the dynamic interactive unity by which two disparate things are held together without loss of their diversity."[9]

While Loder interprets the human spirit as a quality of relationality, I prefer a *capacity* for personal relationality. The change of phrase is intended to reinforce a particular perspective. I want to ascribe an *ontological* dimension to the human spirit. Perhaps the term ontology is a little too precise. Nevertheless, I want to contend that the human spirit is really something rather than a mere *relationship* or an emergent property of brain function. The human person is a self that in relating to the self relates to something: namely, the self that is spirit. If the human person is spirit, the human person as spirit, then, understands itself principally, though not exclusively, through relation with others. The human spirit is not simply an independent autonomous self, but is a self-relating self. C. Stephen Evans comments on Kierkegaard's understanding of the self's relational capacity that is instructive,

> For the self is not just a relation, but a self-relating relation . . . For the self to have a relationship to itself, there must obviously be a duality of sorts in the self. There is the self to whom I am relating and there is the self that is doing the relating. This puzzling concept of the dual self corresponds exactly to our experience. I continually experience myself both as object and as subject.[10]

To assert, then, that the core of human personhood is essentially *spirit* means that the human spirit exists ontologically as

---

8. Legge, *Four Books: Analects of Confucius*, 4:25.
9. Loder and Neidhardt, *Knight's Move*, 10.
10. Evans, *Soren Kierkegaard's Christian Psychology*, 52.

The Humanity of Christ

the ground for relationality and existentially as the experience of self-relatedness with others. It is, however, in the interaction with others that the functional nature of the human person as spirit is revealed.

This interactive-relational capacity of the human spirit, argues Kierkegaard, functions in a context of opposites since the human self is "a synthesis of the infinite and the finite, of the temporal and the eternal, of freedom and necessity." Consequently, the decisive matter for becoming *a self* lies in the nature of the opposites. The opposites, argues Kierkegaard, form the ground for relationality in that they provide the context for a potential shift from being negative, i.e., "a relationship that exists primarily through opposition," to a positive one, i.e., "one that has power in its own right to define the polarities and their relationship."[11] James Loder illustrates the significance of this relational movement between opposites by noting, "The quality of opposition that pertains between male and female and of the love relationship which completes each in, with, and for the other, and is itself transcendent with respect to the opposition [difference] between them."[12]

At first, notes Loder, the opposition or distance of identity appears, but the opposition changes as male and female come to enjoy each other's company and a love relationship develops. The relationship, states Loder, "which was first established on a premise of opposition becomes positive, even a dominant force in the interaction between the two: each increasingly begins to define him/herself in terms of the relationship, per se."[13] In this relationship the polarities of male and female are not lost; rather mutuality heightens individuality.[14] The point of the illustration is that "mutuality becomes a positive third term, not obliterating but intensifying the polarities."[15] Here the pattern of relationality governing "the self as spirit," suggests James Loder, "is perichoretic;

11. Loder and Neidhardt, *Knight's Move*, 290–91.
12. Ibid., 290.
13. Ibid.
14. Ibid.
15. Ibid.

The Nature and Function of the Human Spirit

that is, inner-penetrating," a theologically insightful and helpful concept in grasping the relationality between creaturely existence and the human spirit illustrated by the male/female relationship.[16]

The sexual differentiation between male and female here is analogous of the polarity essential to human personhood which the male and female relationship illustrates. Ray S. Anderson writes, "Personhood is not the result of being male or female. Rather, for the human person, creaturely maleness and femaleness is a manifestation of the fundamental polarity of personhood."[17] James Loder agrees,

> In the mutuality of the polarities, each has the sense that he/she cannot be fully him/herself by him/herself alone, but must have the mutuality in order to continue to be enriched in his/her own particularity.

In this interrelationship the mutuality transcends itself and seeks to place the whole situation in a new context.

If I understand Kierkegaard correctly, it is only when "the self-transcendent agency [the human spirit] of the self finds its ground outside and beyond the pattern of self-relatedness can self-relatedness be sustained."[18] "When the self is "transparently grounded in the power that posits it," writes Loder, "it is, then, *spirit*."[19] What is central here is a relationship of mutual coinherence; that is "opposites are coinherent in and through this relatedness, and the relatedness is coinherent with itself."[20] This entails the interpretation that "the self cannot be itself without its centered grounding beyond itself, but must be a participant in the ground such that its life is preserved and its integrity as spirit is sustained by that ground."[21] Kierkegaard, then, will place the self-relationality

---

16. Ibid.
17. Anderson, *On Being Human*, 106.
18. Ibid., 291.
19. Ibid., 292.
20. Ibid., 291.
21. Ibid., 292.

The Humanity of Christ

of the human person in a unique position between the nature of God and the nature of the human persons as spirit.

At this juncture an important element in the understanding of the relational nature of human persons as spirit enters; namely, "that the self measures itself by the ideal to which it relates itself."[22] C. Stephen Evans comments on this Kierkegaardian perspective. To be a self is to be "a being who is striving toward a certain ideal; this ideal provides the *measure* or *criterion* for the self that is derived from the conscious relationships that have formed the self."[23] While many factors contribute to the person we are and will become (parents, friends, social influences, etc.), genuine selfhood, in the Kierkegaardian perspective, "requires that I stand before God, accepting the self I am as a gift from God and the self I should become as a task God has set for me."[24] Hence, the person that I become emerges from the relational character of the self as the result of the conscious decisions made with reference to the ideal I choose to follow.

C. Stephen Evans offers an excellent example of this important aspect of Kiekegaard's thought:

> A person whose selfhood is completely grounded in his perceived superiority to the slaves he owns fails to be a self. This is so, not because he is not related to other selves—his slaves are persons, but because in regarding the slaves as slaves, the owner does not regard them as genuine selves. Thus, his measure is a defective one, and this infects his own self-conception.[25]

Hence the self is always formed in relation to some ideal. Thus, "the self that lacks God as a conscious ideal will reflect the defective ideal that has replaced God."[26] "What an infinite accent falls on the self," writes Kierkegaard, "by having God as the criterion."[27]

22. Evans, *Kierkegaard's Christian Psychology*, 48.
23. Ibid.
24. Ibid. See also Loder and Neidhardt, *Knight's Move*, 290.
25. Evans, *Kierkegaard's Christian Psychology*, 49.
26. Ibid.
27. Ibid.

The Nature and Function of the Human Spirit

Hence, the human spirit separated from God, the divine Spirit, as its formative ground and ideal becomes dysfunctional and, as a consequence turns in upon itself, reversing the positive relational capacity of the human spirit to a negative, self-centered one.

Pannenberg: The Spiritual Self as an Exocentric Being

The uniqueness of the human person as a relational being finds a compatible voice in Wolfhart Pannenberg. In his book *Anthropology in Theological Perspective*, Pannenberg envisions two major themes essential to an interpretation of the human person; namely, the image of God and human sin.[28] The image of God in human persons, contends Pannenberg, refers to humanity's *closeness* to divine reality, a closeness that also determines humanity's uniqueness in the natural order of creation. This dimension of closeness is central to Pannenberg's interpretation of human nature. He believes that the human person is different from nonhuman creatures in that the dimension of closeness plays a constitutive role in human self-consciousness.[29] This uniqueness or closeness centers in a natural endowment for *ecstasis*; that is, "the standing outside oneself in exocentric centeredness," a phrase that functions as a naturalistic synonym for *spirit*.[30] This exocentric centeredness, notes James Loder, translates into "the built-in human proclivity toward a self-transcendence that is simultaneously self-formative. It is a potentially infinite movement from the person outward that simultaneously feeds back into one's selfhood, yielding internal formation and personal transcendence with respect to the issue at stake."[31] Roger Olson explains Pannenberg' concept of *exocentricity* this way:

---

28. See Pannenberg, *Anthropology in Theological Perspective*, 48, 49, 107.
29. Olson, "Pannenberg's Theological Anthropology," 163.
30. Loder and Neidhardt, *Knight's Move*, 28.
31. Ibid.

The Humanity of Christ

> *Exocentricity* corresponds to the image of God in that humanity is inwardly oriented to an infinite horizon transcending particularity and self-centered existence ... This is mankind's true nature: self-transcendence into unity with a divinely-ordered totality beyond finite, self-enclosed existence.[32]

The exocentric centeredness of human nature, I propose, describes the fundamental function not only of the human spirit but also conversely denotes what is meant by the image of God. James Loder expresses his understanding of exocentric centeredness this way:

> Exocentric centeredness can be conceived of as spirit not merely because it "transcends transformationally," but because it is inherently and irreducibly relational. Just as the Holy Spirit is spoken of as the "go-between God," the human spirit can be spoken of as the go-between image of God in us.[33]

The human spirit, then, is simultaneously exocentric and self-confirming. In other words, while the human spirit constitutes a person's capacity for self-transcendence, it also expresses a powerful drive reaching out in encounter with others in which its transforming force can initiate freedom for positive change. James Loder expressed the thought this way: "The paradox at the core of the human spirit is that such a self-transcending outward move is simultaneously an inward move, reinforcing one's sense of the perichoresis pattern of the self."[34] To possess *spirit*, then, means that humans were created by God to reach out to others in self-affirmation and in so doing gain an understanding of the self as a self-giving being, thereby mirroring the relational nature of Trinitarian personhood of God.

---

32. Olson, "Pannenberg's Theological Anthropology," 163.
33. Loder and Neidhardt, *Knight's Move*, 28.
34. Ibid., 293–94.

The Nature and Function of the Human Spirit

T. F. Torrance: The Human Spirit as the Imago Dei

T. F. Torrance offers additional theological substance to our interpretation by presenting the thesis that in the human sphere, as well as within the divine life, relationality constitutes the reality at stake.[35] Developing his concept of the human person from the personal revelation of God in the incarnation and the interpersonal nature within the Trinitarian personhood of God, Torrance advances a *relational* understanding of the human person created in the image of God. Following the suggestion of Barth, Torrance argues that humans are created in God's image not as solitary individuals, but in human relations in the context as male and female.[36] This relational dimension is not simply a biologically functioning capacity independent of God. Rather, the human person is constituted a relational being basically through a relation with the Creator.[37] This relational understanding of the *imago Dei*, writes Torrance, "is not something that humans possess innately," but is rather dynamic and contingent, for "it is called into existence by a free relation to God and reflects the uncreated relations within God."[38] Torrance clarifies,

> Human beings are held to be the image of God ... not in virtue of our rational nature or of anything we are inherently in our own beings, but solely through a relation to God [by] the grace in which he [God] has brought us in the wholeness and integrity of our [humanness].[39]

The relational capacity of the spirit within the human person, continues Torrance, has its ultimate expression in Jesus Christ, for Jesus "is both the image and reality of God in his incarnate person."[40] This premise entails that "we are not human in virtue of some essence of humanity that we have in ourselves but only

---

35. Torrance, "Goodness and Dignity," 315–18.
36. Torrance, "Soul and Person, 108–9.
37. Ibid., 109.
38. Torrance, *Christian Frame of Mind*, 38.
39. Torrance, "Goodness and Dignity," 317.
40. Ibid.

The Humanity of Christ

in virtue of what we received from his [Christ's] humanity which embodies the Life that is the Light of humanity."[41] "We are," argues Torrance, "personalized persons who draw from him [Christ] the true substance of our personal being both in relation to God and in relation to one another."[42] It is only by reference to what Christ is that we must think of humans as created in the image of God.

Noting that the Greek Patristic Fathers viewed the human person in a non-dualistic way, Torrance contends that the Greek Patristic Fathers offered little, if any, psychological analysis of the human person as body, soul and spirit. Torrance, therefore, interprets the human person "in body and soul as related to God through the power and presence of the divine Spirit and thereby endowed with the capacity to think and act in accordance with the nature of what is other than himself."[43]

Consequently, contends Torrance, the human spirit does not denote a *third thing* in the human person along with body and soul, but refers to a "transcendental determination of his existence in soul and body, constituting him as a human being before God in relation to other human beings."[44] Humans, therefore, do not possess a spirit as "an ingredient or potency in his/her make-up, or as a *'spark of the divine.'*"[45] Rather, contends Torrance, the human spirit is "the ontological qualification of his soul, and indeed of his/her whole creaturely being," as human persons made in the image and likeness of God brought about by the initial work of the divine Creator Spirit.[46]

When Torrance speaks of *transcendental determination* of the human spirit, he does not understand this in a deterministic manner, but rather in terms of the personalizing and humanizing activity of God that respects and grounds the human creature in freedom. Torrance writes,

41. Ibid., 318.
42. Torrance, *Christian Frame*, 39.
43. Torrance, "Goodness and Dignity," 317.
44. Torrance, "Soul and Person," 110.
45. Ibid.
46. Ibid.

The Nature and Function of the Human Spirit

> While the spirit of man . . . is not to be regarded as an inherent feature of his being along with his soul and body, nevertheless it is owing to his being spirit or having spirit that man is sharply differentiated from all other animated bodies in the creation as rational beings made *ad imaginem Dei*. In this event he may be understood not from an independent center in himself but only from above and beyond himself in his transcendental relation to God.[47]

This, of course, does not mean that the human person is called to embrace a process of deification through participation in the essence of God. Rather, it means "a distinctive transcendental determination of his being for God which both confirms it in its creaturely reality as utterly different from God and adapts man in his contingent nature of knowledge of God and fellowship with [God]."[48]

The uniqueness of the human person, then, lies in his/her relational capacity as the consequence of the possession of spirit. It is this perspective of the relational capacity of humans that Pringle-Pattison differentiated the Christian conception of the world in contrast to the Hellenic view in that the Christian conception of reality "regards persons and the relations of persons to one another as the essence of reality."[49] Torrance describes this relational reality as constituting the

> free, dynamic, relational and personal character of God and the contingent, free, dynamic and relational character of creaturely reality, including human beings, where creaturely reality becomes personal [both] in relation to God" and others.[50]

This capacity for personal, free, relationality within creaturely existence is what constitutes the image of God in the human person, a capacity inaugurated and enabled by the possession of a

---

47. Ibid.
48. Torrance, *Christian Frame*, 319.
49. Pringle-Pattison, *Idea of God*, 291.
50. Torrance, *Christian Frame*, 39.

human spirit who unites us to Christ and through Christ with the Father, and will bring our creaturely relations to their true end and fulfillment in union and communion with the triune God.[51]

George Hendry: The Human Spirit as a Gift and Object of Divine Grace

Few scholars are better suited to address the freedom of the human spirit as an object of divine grace than George S. Hendry in his helpful and insightful book *The Holy Spirit in Christian Theology*. In his chapter on the "The Holy Spirit and the Human Spirit," Hendry discusses a specific concern with his own Reformed theological tradition. His concern is that Reformed theology's stress on *sola gratia* has done a disservice in minimizing the significance of the human spirit.[52] If persons are redeemed by grace alone, writes Hendry, there is, then, "left no need of correlation with anything on the part of man."[53] Grace alone by its nature infers a total incapacity on the part of man to discover or to achieve any contact with God. Hendry asserts,

> The knowledge of God [in Reformed theology] is made to depend so exclusively on the down-reach of the divine Spirit that any movement of up-reach on the part of the human spirit can be construed only as an attempt to bypass [grace alone].[54]

The consequence of this theological perspective, continues Hendry, "was that the spirit of man was not brought into a positive relation with the Spirit of God in faith; and man was to all intents and purposes *de-spirited*."[55] Consequently, the human spirit in Reformed theology plays no role in an encounter with God. The human spirit is understood as spiritually dead, and, therefore, its

---

51. Torrance, "Goodness and Dignity," 317–18.
52. Hendry, *Holy Spirit in Christian Theology*, 99.
53. Ibid., 98.
54. Ibid., 99.
55. Ibid., 100.

The Nature and Function of the Human Spirit

part is one of complete passivity. The Reformed understanding of divine sovereignty and the sufficiency of grace, concludes Hendry, "left no room for human effort or even for human aspiration. The *agape* motif dominated the picture so completely, that *eros* was eliminated altogether."[56]

Hendry seeks to overcome this neglect of the human spirit by reflecting on the incarnation. In the incarnation, notes Hendry, two aspects of grace can be observed. The first element that dominated the understanding of grace in the Reformers is *condescension*. Condescension denotes that dimension of grace in which the eternal God reaches down in Christ Jesus to reconcile sinful humanity. Through his death as an atoning sacrifice, Christ establishes a relationship of peace between God and human beings. In actualizing this status of peace, it is the totality of grace that dominates the entire redemptive process. Martin Luther concurs,

> I believe that I cannot by my own reason or power believe in Jesus Christ my Lord or come to him; but the Holy Spirit has called me through the gospel, enlightened me with his gifts, sanctified and preserved me in the true faith.[57]

While Reformed theologian John Calvin sought to give a place to the human spirit in his thought, Henry contends that he falls short. Since humanity is totally sinful, this entails, argues Calvin, that the human nature, and conversely the human spirit, is perverted and corrupted. Consequently, the knowledge of God depends exclusively on the down-reach of the divine Spirit so that any movement of reach on the part of the human spirit is antithetical to God's sovereign movement of grace.[58] Even when persons are brought to the knowledge of God through God's Word and Spirit, the human spirit still plays little or no part. Though Calvin predicates an active human spirit but only of the converted man,[59]

---

56. Ibid.
57. Luther, *Small Catechism*, WA 7,550, cited by Hendry, *Holy Spirit*, 98.
58. Hendry, *Holy Spirit*, 99.
59. Calvin, *Institutes*, 689.

The Humanity of Christ

even here contends Hendry, "the human spirit is totally dependent upon the transforming activity of the Holy Spirit for any renewing of human nature."[60]

The second element of grace noted by Hendry is *accommodation*. This dimension of grace, contends Hendry, was neglected in Reformed theology because of "the mistake of equating *indispensable with irresistible*."[61] Hendry, therefore, argues that "the humanity to whom God accommodates is humanity as endowed with a created spirit, the hallmark of which is human freedom."[62] Hendry's contention is that the grace of God "does not override human freedom; it respects it; it engages it to the full extent, it bows before it, because that is the only way in which a [genuine] real relation, i.e., a personal relation between God and [humankind] can be realized."[63] The absence of human freedom due to the concept of irresistible grace, argues Hendry, can only establish an I-It relation and could not create a I-Thou relationship so essential to relationship with a personal God. To effect a personal relationship, a person must be encountered as a Thou, i.e., as a subject whose freedom is respected.[64]

When Christ took on human nature, God affirms humanity; that is, God subsumes the divine being in Christ under humanity. In the divine condescension, writes Hendry, "God subjects Christology to anthropology."[65] If I have understood Hendry correctly, the humanity affirmed is essentially the freedom enabled by the possession of spirit. Hendry writes,

> The Holy Spirit does not annihilate our spirits, but bears witness with our spirits. And the Holy Spirit does not destroy the freedom of our spirit, but restores it by changing [its] false freedom from God into that true freedom

---

60. Hendry, *Holy Spirit in Christian Theology*, 98.
61. Ibid., 112.
62. Ibid., 113.
63. Ibid.
64. Ibid.
65. Ibid.

The Nature and Function of the Human Spirit

for God, which is "the glorious liberty of the children of God."[66]

In other words, divine grace redirects the function of the human spirit away from its egotistical distortion back into a positive trust-relationship with God. Hendry argues that a relationship with God requires a relationship of Spirit-to-spirit, or freedom-to freedom.[67] God does not dehumanize humanity in the offer of divine grace. Rather, God orients the human spirit back to submit to its proper object; namely, God.

James Loder's comment on reinterpreting irresistible grace is very helpful. Loder writes,

> Irresistible grace needs to be reinterpreted as a grace whose keynote is nonresistance; God does not overrule human freedom but engages it in order that the I-Thou of the God-human relationship [is] not reduced to the I-it order . . . When grace enters the situation, the disoriented human spirit is not destroyed by grace; it is transformed so that it may choose freely to testify with God's Spirit that we are the children of God. Thus, the impact of grace on the human spirit is to awaken it to a true sense of its freedom to be itself as image restored to its original.[68]

In formulating a biblical and contemporary doctrine of the human spirit, we must, therefore, never devalue nor minimize the importance of the biblical teaching that the Son of God became human (Heb 10:5; Phil 2:7–8) and dwelt among us (John 1:14). The author to the Epistle Hebrews clearly points to the importance of Jesus' humanity when he wrote, "When Christ came into the world, he said: Sacrifice and offering you did not desire, but a *body* you prepared for me" (Heb 10:5). Although Christ existed in the very divine nature of God, he did not desperately grasp on to the revelatory glory of divine status but relinquished it, humbly

---

66. Ibid., 117.
67. Ibid., 115.
68. Loder, *Logic of the Spirit*, 34–35.

The Humanity of Christ

condescending to clothe himself with a genuine human nature (Phil 2:6–8).

Christ clothed himself with a human nature to be a sin offering for us (Rom 8:3) so that "both the one who makes men holy and those who are made holy are of the same family" (Heb 2:11). Christ sanctified human nature in himself and was divinely transformed into what the New Testament calls the power of an indestructible life (Heb 7:16). Through the hypostatic union of the divine and human natures, Christ assumed our broken and alienated humanity without himself becoming contaminated by our fallen condition, creating a union that enabled him to condemn sin in our sinful humanity and to overcome the estrangement, of sin and death entrenched in our humanity.

Christ embodied the tensions and contradictions of our sinful and rebellious humanity in such a way, writes T. F. Torrance, that "his atoning reconciliation not only takes dynamic form but is also worked out within actual historical relations and structures of our human existence through his life, death, resurrection and ascension" of Christ our Lord.[69]

This atoning reconciliation, however, continues Torrance, "could not be actualized without overcoming human sin and guilt through the atoning death of Christ and through the sanctification of our human nature." Moreover, an *atoning exchange* "could not take place within the depths of our alienated and [dysfunctional] humanity unless Christ penetrated into those depths in the hypostatic union between Christ's divine and human nature."[70]

Divine grace, therefore, initiated both a downward movement of divine love for sinful humanity and at the same time offers an upward movement in Jesus Christ by which humanity is opened to God and the human spirit enters into the process of its healing through reconciliation with God. Karl Barth reflects on this double aspect of Christ's redemptive work.

---

69. Torrance, *Mediation of Christ*, 85.
70. Ibid.

The Nature and Function of the Human Spirit

> In Jesus Christ there is no isolation of man from God or of God from man . . . [Jesus Christ] is the Word spoken from the loftiest . . . transcendence and likewise the Word heard in the deepest, darkest immanence. . . [Jesus Christ] attests and guarantees to man God's free grace and at the same time attests and guarantees to God man's free gratitude.[71]

Thus, divine grace is both the source and the initiator by which human persons may enter into personal relationship with God and the human spirit may experience its true ground and meaning in a restored relationship with triune God and the divine Spirit.

---

71. Barth, *Humanity of God*, 46.

3

The Dysfunction of the Human Spirit

INTRODUCTION

THAT HUMANS LIVE IN a tension between what we *are* and what we *ought* to be seems an obvious deduction, a conclusion documented at both the personal and phenomenological levels. Our newspapers and television news broadcasts, for example, constantly report how we as humans act in selfish, arrogant, and cruel ways and how the powerful in both governments and social groups justify injustice against the weak and powerless out of self-interest. While humans clearly do good deeds, these deeds are eclipsed by the overwhelming acts of violence and cruelty perpetrated against others—the rape of women, the atrocities committed by soldiers, the abuse of children, etc. Indeed, the inhumanity that humans impose upon other humans far exceeds the cruelty within the realm of nonhuman creatures. It has been said that "humans, the only animal addicted to perpetual war upon its own kind, are not

The Dysfunction of the Human Spirit

only ethically inferior to the most frightful beasts but also lives in more disorder and violence than any known animal."[1]

The biblical tradition places the primary source of this dysfunction in the loss of relationship with God and the resultant consequence in which humanity is placed under the dictatorial and distorting power of sin. David, the Psalmist, declares, "Behold, I was brought forth in iniquity" (Ps 51:5). Here David acknowledges a deep disorder exists within human nature. "It is as though some dreadful thing," comments Ray Anderson, "has attached itself to the core of his being and he can neither shake it loose nor forget it."[2] The Apostle Paul also testifies to malady of sin lodged in the core of human personhood. He describes the tragic deterioration of humans as humane creatures as the result of humanity's idolatrous rejection of God the Creator. The Apostle Paul writes,

> Since they did not think it worthwhile to retain the knowledge of God, he [God] *gave them over* to a depraved mind . . . They [humanity] have become filled with every kind of wickedness, evil, greed and depravity. They are full of envy, murder, strife, deceit and malice. They are gossips, slanderers, God-haters, insolent, arrogant and boastful; they invent ways of doing evil; they disobey their parents; they are senseless, faithless, heartless, and ruthless. (Rom 1:29–31)

Paul's point is clear. Humanity's broken relationship with God has resulted in the loss of the truly human. This separation involves not only the loss of divine presence but also the eclipse of the sacred order, "the twin causes," writes Albert C. Outler, "of our dehumanization."[3] The problem of sin, therefore, entails both a *theological problem* (the loss of relationship with God) as well as a *personal-human problem* (the dysfunction of human personhood).

These two dimensions, however, should not be taken as mutually exclusive issues. They are, in fact, inseparably connected. An integral connection exists within humanity between human

---

1. Carmichael, *Sin and Forgiveness*, 111.
2. Anderson, *On Being Human*, 3.
3. Outler, "Loss of the Sacred," 17.

The Humanity of Christ

creatureliness and the unique spiritual dimension of human existence. The two are bound together by the creative act of God in which humans stand before God not only as creatures but also as human persons created to function as *persons-in-community*. Hence, theologian Dale Moody writes,

> Modern man has often turned away from the mystery of God only to find himself a mystery almost as great, for he is unable to understand himself apart from his relation to God.[4]

The present task of this chapter, then, is to discuss the assertion that sin is both a theological and a personal-human problem in the context of the command to be holy as God is holy. It is not the purpose here to examine the multiplicity of proposed theological-biblical definitions of sin, nor the various metaphors by which the several definitions of sin are explicated. Rather, by proposing that an inseparable connection exists between human creatureliness and the unique spiritual capacity within human personhood, the interpretations of sin that involve these two components will be the primary focus, especially as they contribute to our understanding of the command to be holy as God is holy. The question of sin becomes relevant in view of the proposed premise that the human spirit has become dysfunctional not only due to the entrance of sin into human existence but also that our concept of sin impacts our view of the Christian life.

SIN AS HUMAN IMPERFECTION

The early Greek philosophers taught that sin finds its source in the limitations of human creatureliness; that is, in human ignorance and finitude. Arguing that humans were originally created as immortal, pure, spirit-souls, existing in perfect communion with God in an eternal spirit world, these eternal spirit-souls became subjected to physical, temporal existence as the consequence of some disobedience in that spirit-world. As a consequence, humans

---

4. Moody, *Word of Truth*, 16.

The Dysfunction of the Human Spirit

were cast out of the spirit-world and subjected to a state of imperfection and death. It is this embodied existence that is the source of sinful acts since existence is now susceptible to the temptations issuing from the demands and desire of creatureliness. It is only with the release from physical and temporal existence that deliverance or salvation can occur. Hence, from this perspective death assumes soteriological significance.

Sin as Human Limitations: Tennant and Schleiermacher

A different, yet generally compatible, viewpoint is found in the writings of Frederick R. Tennant. Tennant argues that the source of sin lies in our animal nature.[5] It is the result of instincts and patterns of behavior arising from our ancestral origins that continues to persist into the advanced periods of the evolutionary process until humans acquire moral consciousness; that is, moral sensitivity or awareness. The evolutionary process, Tennant believed, would eventually produce a dominant sense of moral awareness within humans. With the advancement of this moral-ethical consciousness, our primitive animal instincts could, then, be controlled and moral-ethical patterns of behavior would prevail.

Fredrick Schleiermacher also advances this understanding of sin, but with the insertion of the component of God-consciousness; that is, the awareness of all things dependent upon God. While identifying the source of sin with the Pauline concept of the *flesh* which he interprets as "the totality of the so-called lower powers of the soul,"[6] he contrasts the *flesh* with his concept of the *spirit* that denotes humanity's *higher* or moral propensities that emerge with God-consciousness. It is in the conflict between the lower and higher powers of human experience that sin occurs. In essence, sin is the result of the powerful desires and passions of physical existence in the absence or incapacity of the spirit. Schlei-

---

5. Tennant, *Origin and Propagation of Sin*, 114.
6. Schleiermacher, *On Christian faith*, 271.

The Humanity of Christ

ermacher writes, "We are conscious of sin as the power and work at a time when the disposition to the God-consciousness had not yet actively emerged in us."[7] Or stated from a different perspective, sin is an arrestment of the determinative power of the spirit, due to the independence or power of the sensuous desires.[8]

Sin, then, arises as the consequence of undeveloped spiritual-moral awareness within the evolutionary moral development of humanity. At this undeveloped stage, there is no resistance to the sinful urges of the flesh; that is, the passions of our natural-physical existence. These fleshly acts, however, are not sin in the proper sense, but simply constitute the *germ of sin* since the functions of the lower life are developed prior to God-consciousness. Because creaturely existence involves self-preservation, this mode of self-centeredness is essential for the survival of the evolving human creature. Without a spiritual awareness, sin, in the technical sense, does not exist, asserts Schleiermacher. It is only with the emergence of God-consciousness and the ascendancy of the spirit that the moral power of the will emerges, enabling us to resist the temptations of our lower passions.

Sin, therefore, emerges from the act of confining human existence exclusively to self-centered survival, that is, to the experience of pleasure and pain, and to resisting the urge to transcend creatureliness through the emergence of a spiritual awareness (feeling of absolute dependence) of all things on God-consciousness. This means that, for Schleiermacher, creatureliness does not possess within itself the power for overcoming the tension between the "is" and the "ought" of human existence. It is this tension between what humans "are" (creaturely beings) and how humans "ought" to think and act (the power of the spirit) that forms the emergence for sin and evil in Schleiermacher's religious thought. The essence of sin then is, for Schleiermacher, "the yielding of the self's identity to the vacillation of the pleasant and unpleasant moments in the world through its sensible self-consciousness."[9]

7. Ibid., 273.
8. Ibid., 275.
9. Ibid.

The Dysfunction of the Human Spirit

With the emergence of God-consciousness, however, comes a new understanding of the world. The world is now viewed in terms of the interconnectedness of all things dependent on God. With the emergence of God-consciousness a reversal of orientation occurs that transcends the passions of physicality. Put in terms of *goodness*, Schleiermacher appears at times to view sin as the incapacity for good—good being understood solely as that which is determined by God-consciousness.[10] Sin, therefore, is simply the failure *to take command of one's self*,[11] to embrace the moral goodness God-consciousness urges humans to express.

The God-consciousness to which Schleiermacher refers is the *feeling of absolute dependence* that constitutes the highest grade of human self-consciousness. It denotes not only a self-consciousness that recognizes the necessity to transcend the self-centeredness of survival but also awakens the awareness of the interdependence of all things under God and the moral conduct this feeling of dependence obligates.

It is only with the coming of the Redeemer, contends Schleiermacher, that humanity is brought to God-consciousness and achieves its release from its imprisonment to sin. The redeemer, who is God, is capable of actualizing that which humanity sorely needs. But also being human, the Redeemer fits into the interconnectedness of all finite existence so that which the Redeemer, who is Christ, accomplishes becomes a fact of existence that affects all. That is, the Redeemer lives a life of perfect God-consciousness, thereby establishing a reality, like leaven in a loaf, that will eventually mediate that God-consciousness to the rest of humanity.

Richard R. Niebuhr sums up Schleiermacher's view of the work of Christ, the Redeemer, as follows:

> The Redeemer is a teacher of a new doctrine about God that Christ proffers to others. What he gives is the power of God in the embodiment of his own ideal humanity and . . . as the source from which men may receive that power. Schleiermacher advances two aspects of Jesus'

10. Ibid., 283.
11. Ibid.

The Humanity of Christ

work which he calls his Urbildichkeit [ideality] and his Vorbildlichkeit [exemplarity] that cannot be separated. By virtue of the former he is the Redeemer; by virtue of the latter he communicates redemption. Therefore, while the Vorbildichkeit or exemplary status of Jesus does not signify his life-giving power as the Redeemer appointed eternally by God, it does signify his solidarity with the human race, apart from which there could be no communication of redemption.[12]

James Livingston interprets Schleiermacher's view of the work of the Redeemer this way:

> The work of Christ in redemption consists in the implanting of God-consciousness as the dominant principle life, thereby gaining the victory over the sensuous impulses and ordering human consciousness in such a way that pain and melancholy give way to a new sense of equilibrium and joy, a new attunement of the soul in its relation to God and the world.[13]

Sin as Personal Conflict: Lower and Higher Dimensions of Human Nature

A final—and perhaps more insightful—viewpoint can be found in the writings of Reinhold Niebuhr. Niebuhr is more compelling in my opinion because he seeks to coordinate in a meaningful way the creaturely dimension of human personhood and the theological in his interpretation of sin. In *The Nature and Destiny of Man*, Niebuhr interprets the significance of human beings from a divine perspective; that is, from the standpoint of relationship with God rather than simply in terms of the limitations and/or potentials of human creatureliness. At the same time, however, Niebuhr interprets the human rejection of God in the context of an existential anxiety arising out of the human condition of every human person.

---

12. Niebuhr, *Schleiermacher on Christ and Religion*, 226.
13. Livingston and Fiorenza, *Modern Christian Thought*, 1:103.

The Dysfunction of the Human Spirit

Because humans are finite creatures, and yet, at the same time, possess a human spirit, humans experience the tension, reasons Niebuhr, of being bound as the result of creatureliness while, on the other hand, the experience of being free as the result of the possession of the human spirit. While not divorced from creatureliness, the human spirit here denotes the human capacity to transcend human embodiment and consequently its appetites and passions. Hence, Niebuhr asserts that the human spirit in its depth and height reaches into eternity and that this vertical dimension is more important for the understanding of human personhood than merely his rational capacity or the forming general concepts. This height is none other than the human capacity to transcend not only the self, but also the world, gaining an eternal perspective derived from God-consciousness.

The spirit-capacity to transcend human finiteness, however, creates a state of existential anxiety from which the temptation to sin emerges. Niebuhr writes,

> In his anxiety, he [human persons] seeks to transmute his finiteness into infinity, his weakness into strength, his dependence into independence. He seeks, in other words, to escape finiteness and weakness by a quantitative rather than a qualitative development of his life. The quantitative antithesis of finiteness is infinity. The qualitative possibility of human life is its obedient subjection to the will of God.[14]

Sin, then, emerges from allowing one's natural existence to usurp the role of the spirit and thereby sets itself up as its own master or arbiter, defining the limits and securing the self as if one's own limited perspective was in fact absolute. Consequently, creaturely existence assumes an absolute defining role, ignoring the freedom of the spirit. Hence, for Niebuhr, sin can be defined as either sensuality or pride. Both constitute the motivation for the emergence of a self-centered existence that defines the essence of sin. In this existential dynamic, sin is encountered by every human being as ultimately rebellion against God. Hence, the theological

---

14. Niebuhr, *Nature and Destiny of Man*, 251.

The Humanity of Christ

dimension of the spirit plays a fundamental role in Niebuhr's definition of the tension with sin in human existence.

Niebuhr's interpretation of sin, I believe, is unique among those who find a connection between human creatureliness and sin. Its uniqueness lies in his recognition of the significance of human creatureliness and his attempt to coordinate this aspect with human freedom and responsibility arising from his view of the spirit. Whether Niebuhr's view is convincing or not, one critical perspective stands out for the concern of this book; namely, that the significance of human creatureliness should not be dismissed in formulating a view of the unique spiritual dimension and calling to which humans are bound.

While adopting a different perspective, I, nevertheless, find Niebuhr's stress on the power of the spirit to overcome the drives and passions of creatureliness and to promote moral and humane conduct insightful. I will argue later that the possession of the human spirit, if healed of its dysfunction, motivates, directs, and influences the natural functions of human creatures in moral-ethical and humane behavior. Unfortunately, with the dominance of *totalis gratis* in the theology of the Reformers and much of Protestant Evangelical theology, the role of the human spirit has become completely passive. No place is left for the correlation on the part of the human spirit with the divine Spirit. There is only total incapacity for the human spirit. This perspective correlates with the interpretation that all persons possess a sinful-guilty nature inherited from Adam, leaving human personhood, as George Hendry contends, essentially "*de-spirited.*" While finding some insightful thoughts in Niebuhr's interpretation, attempts to locate the source of sin in the limitations and imperfections of human creatureliness are not convincing. Consider some of the following reasons.

(1) A difficulty encountered by the position that human creatureliness is the primary source of sinful acts lies in its inability to account adequately for the diversity of human evil. The evil perpetuated by humans is far too complex and extensive in its expressions to be limited to human creatureliness. From the sin of Cain to the modern cruelty and violence initiated,

The Dysfunction of the Human Spirit

for example, by such persons as Adolf Hilter, Pol Pot, or Milosevic, to say nothing of the greed and desire for status and power evident in structural sin, indicates that a creaturely basis for sin does not provide a sufficient answer. Nor does it appear to be the case that the evolutionary process has lessened in any significant way the enormity and frequent pointlessness of human misdeeds. Something more than creatureliness is at work.

(2) A second difficulty centers in the fact that natural desires are not in themselves sinful; at least, not in the original creative purposes of God. The desires of human creatureliness were created by God for the benefit and pleasure of humans. If this is the case, is it not reasonable to conclude that these natural desires have come under the control of other forces—forces that pervert them toward improper thinking and acting, resulting in various selfish and inhumane acts? Moreover, since human violence continues unabated to the present, is it not legitimate to ask how much longer must humanity linger in the evolutionary-developmental process for this higher level of moral awareness to alter human conduct in a significant way? Something other than creatureliness seems to be at work, conscripting creaturely capacity for inhumane and evil purposes.

(3) Third, it seems logical to hold the view that moral responsibility does not naturally arise from within creatureliness but is imposed upon creaturely existence by means of some external criterion, such as God, the value of human life, the necessity of civil order, natural law, etc. Contrary to Kant's insistence that morality must be autonomous, I would argue with Professor John Smith, that no view of the moral life, no serious doctrine of what humans ought to do, can be sustained apart from some transcendent reference to which it is itself subject and judged.[15]

---

15. Smith, *Reason and God*, 200–201.

The Humanity of Christ

(4) Fourth, from a theological-biblical perspective, it could be argued that if creatureliness is the source of our distortion and alienation, Jesus Christ as God could not have assumed human existence without simultaneously assuming or taking upon himself the presence of sin. Hence, the biblical declaration "God made him to be sin who *had no sin*" (2 Cor 5:21) would be a false assertion. It appears, then, that a compelling case for sinful actions lies elsewhere.[/NL]

While finding some insightful reflections in Niebuhr's interpretation, the attempts to locate the source of sin in the limitations of human creatureliness are not convincing. We will, therefore, turn our attention to a theological-biblical interpretation that has dominated much of the Protestant Evangelical Church since the Reformation—an interpretation that owes much of its seminal theological formulation to the influence and teachings of Augustine and John Calvin.

AN AUGUSTINIAN-CALVINIST INTERPRETATION

Drawing on Genesis 3:1–24 and Romans 5:12–19 as the most explicit biblical accounts of the emergence of original sin into the human experience, a widely accepted Protestant-Evangelical position, briefly stated, is that the origin of sin finds its source in Adam's free act of disobedience. This act of disobedience centered in the rejection of God's gracious and protecting command, *Do not eat of the tree*. The consequence of this rejection resulted not only in a rupture of relationship between God and humankind but also in the loss of *original goodness*. With the loss of *original goodness*, there was imputed to humankind an ontological propensity toward sin. An *irrevocable corruption* now exists within the core of every human person, distorting the spiritual capacity of all humankind. This interpretation is in part deduced from the words of the Apostle Paul recorded in Romans 5:12. The text reads, "Therefore, just as sin entered the world through one man, and death through sin, and in this way death came to all men, *because all sinned*" (Rom

The Dysfunction of the Human Spirit

5:12). Recognizing that the passage centers on the *consequence* of Adam's disobedience upon all persons rather than on the actual sins people commit, it is argued that an inseparable connection now exists between the disobedience of the *one* man, Adam, and the *many* resulting in the imputation of guilt, condemnation, and corruption upon *all* humankind. That the sinful-guilty-corrupt nature of the *one* man was imputed to the *many* primarily centers on an interpretation of the phrase, *because all have sinned* (Rom 5:12). John Calvin, for example, interprets this phrase "because all have sinned" from Romans 5:12b to mean that there is imputed to all humankind an inherited depravity and corruption of their human nature.

> Original sin . . . [is] an hereditary depravity and corruption of our nature, diffused through all the parts of the soul, . . . because we are all subject to a curse, in consequence of his [Adam's] transgression, . . . producing in us those works which the Scripture calls *works of the flesh*, . . . He [Adam] is therefore said to have involved us in guilt.[16]

Wayne Grudem, a contemporary proponent, succinctly expresses the position:

> This idea that "*all men sinned*" means that God thought of us all [humankind] as having sinned when Adam disobeyed.[17]

As a result of Adam's disobedience, this interpretation finds in Romans 5:12–19 three consequences that can be deduced from Adam's original sin that are immediately imputed upon humankind. First, death came upon all persons. The biblical text reads, "For, if by the trespass of the one man, death reigned through that one man" (Rom 5:17). Second, condemnation was imputed upon all persons, "Just as the result of one trespass was condemnation for all men" (Rom 5:17). Third, as a consequence of the one man's disobedience, all persons are constituted (or regarded) as sinners.

---

16. Calvin, *Institutes*, 251.
17. Grudem, *Systematic Theology*, 494.

The Humanity of Christ

The text again reads, "For just as through the disobedience of the one man, the many were constituted [regarded as] sinners" (Rom 5:19).

That all persons are constituted sinners, existing under divine judgment and separated from personal fellowship with God, does not, however, determine the particular mode of the connection between the one sin of Adam and the divine judgment upon the human race. It is, therefore, proposed that Adam functioned as the *representative head* of humankind. The biblical text reads, "sin entered the world through one man" with the consequence that "in Adam all sinned" (Rom 5:12). The conclusion is, therefore, deduced that all persons possess a *sinful-guilty nature* inherited from Adam who functioned not only as the *seminal origin* of humankind, but also as the *representative head* of the human race, imputing to all humankind the consequence of his representative act of disobedience (Rom 5:12b). Through seminal and representative headship, humankind has become joint-sharers in the consequences of Adam's sin since all humankind has their ancestral origin and seminal nature in Adam.

It is, however, historically speaking, interesting to note that prior to the third century, the interpretation of imputed guilt for original sin had not yet become an established doctrine of the Christian church. The writings of the Patristic Fathers and the early Apologists generally focused on the significance of redemption and did so predominately with the Christological premise in which Christ snatches sinners from the grasp of Satan. It is not until the emergence of the theology of Augustine in the 4th century that a definitive connection is made between the one sin of Adam and the imputed guilt and ontological corruption of humankind, though several of Augustine's key premises can be found in seminal form in the writings of Tertullian and Origen. The interpretation of Augustine, refined and advanced by John Calvin, continues as a preferred interpretation of original sin within much of the Evangelical Protestant Church today.

The question, nevertheless, persists, have we understood Paul's meaning in Romans 5:12–19 correctly? Did Paul teach in

The Dysfunction of the Human Spirit

this passage that human nature is totally corrupt and thus incapable of responding to God's gift of grace in Christ? Or did Paul teach that the judgment of Adam's sin brought *death* into the world with all of its decaying effects, not an ontological corruption? In other words, is the interpretation that all persons possess a *sinful-corrupt* nature from Adam's one act of disobedience the more accurate interpretation of Paul's words in Romans 5:12–19? If all persons possess a *sinful-corrupt nature* that dominates human conduct, are not the several biblical commands to be holy as God is holy, then, not only an unachievable but also a deceptive command? If all persons are ontologically corrupt in nature and will continue to be so until the consummation of all things, how, then, will believers be able to fulfill the commands to live godly lives as God requires? This question is a critical one for any believer striving to live the Christian life as God demands.

THE DYSFUNCTION OF THE HUMAN SPIRIT
An Alternative Interpretation

While the traditional Augustinian-Calvinist view presents a logically compelling interpretation of the Romans 5:12–19 passage, several concerns persist.

(1) To propose an inherited corrupt nature imputed from Adam's one act of disobedience independent from personal involvement diminishes the biblical emphasis on personal responsibility. Guilt is not normally imputed separate from personal accountability. Since a judicial category, such as the imputation of Adam's sin, does not require an individual act of transgression, on what basis, then, did those persons who did not sin in the likeness of Adam's transgression but nevertheless were held accountable for some kind of transgressions independent of Adam, experienced divine judgment of death (Rom 5:13). Since they did not sin as Adam, what did they do that caused divine judgment to be placed upon them? Was their sin somehow a personal transgression?

The Humanity of Christ

(2) The historical reference to the persons who lived between Adam and Moses when the law did not exist (Rom 5:13–14) raise the same issue but from a different perspective. *For where there is no law*, states Paul, sin is not imputed (5:13). Nevertheless, we read that *death* reigned, even over these specific persons in this historical reference who did not sin as Adam did. Since these persons experienced the judgment of physical death as a consequence of some personal misdeed that was in some way different from that of Adam's transgression, is Paul, then, simply teaching that these persons, who did not sin as Adam did, but, nevertheless, experienced divine judgment in terms of physical death, imply that there were some persons who experienced divine judgment due to their own personal act(s) of sin? The key thought here is that they did not sin as Adam did, suggesting that their transgression was in some sense independent of or different from Adam's transgression. The question, then, arises, what sin did these persons commit that constitutes the basis of the divine judgment of death?

(3) Since the notion of total corruption does not explicitly occur in Romans 5:12–19, is it not reasonable to assume that Paul is simply making an argument from the correlation between *death* and *life* as the results of the respective acts of Adam and Christ with reference to humankind? Paul clearly makes this emphasis elsewhere. He writes, "For as in Adam all die, so in Christ all will be made alive" (1 Cor 15:22). And then again in Romans 5:17, "For if, by the trespass of the one man, death reigned through that one man, how much more will those who receive God's abundant provision of grace and of the gift of righteousness reign in life through the one man, Jesus Christ."

(4) One final thought. While there are several grammatical issues associated with Romans 5:12b, we need to take care in interpreting the use of the aorist tense of the verb "sinned" in the key phrase "all have sinned" (Rom 5:12b) since the

The Dysfunction of the Human Spirit

aorist tense permits various interpretative stresses. For our present concern, consider the nearest parallel to the aorist verbal use of *sinned* in Romans 5:12b found in the Septuagint text of Leviticus 4:3.[18] In Leviticus 4:3 the verb "to sin," notes Henri Blocher, "is used in the aorist tense for the people's state of *asam* [penalty] in consequence of the high priest's fault."[19] However, since the verb "to sin," *hamartein*, continues Blocher, "rarely corresponds to *asam*, the notion of *asam*, then, may not lead us far beyond a mere penalty or judgment undergone as a result of the high priest's fault—not [personal] guilt incurred."[20][/NL]

It may be helpful at this point to propose that the New Testament imputes divine judgment on two levels. The first level constitutes a *corporate level*; that is, divine judgment is imputed upon all humanity as a consequence of seminal union with Adam. *Death*, therefore, can come upon all persons independent of personal acts of sin. Here Paul's stress on the relationship of the One and the Many is upheld. Secondly, divine judgment is also imputed on a personal level. Personal judgment is imputed on the basis of an individual act(s) of sin. The occurrence of judgment cited in Romans 5:14 when persons did not sin by breaking a command as did Adam implies that those who did not sin like Adam's sinned, but nevertheless have personally sinned in some manner, provides a potential example of the personal level of accountability.

There is, I believe, a correlation between these two events. The persons who did not sin as Adam sinned and consequently experienced the divine judgment of death, also have the basis of their judgment in the rejection (a failure to trust) in God's Lordship as sovereign Creator as Adam did. They also transferred allegiance and worship away from God the Creator to the creatures of creation. The Apostle Paul explains,

---

18. Blocher, *Original Sin*, 73.
19. Ibid.
20. Ibid.

The Humanity of Christ

> For although they [humankind] knew God, they neither glorified him as God nor gave thinks to him, but their thinking became futile and their foolish hearts were darkened Although they claimed to be wise, they became fools and exchanged the glory of the immortal God for images made to look like mortal human beings and birds and animal and reptiles. Therefore, God gave them over. (Rom 1:21–24a)

The New Testament contains a clear emphasis on individual human responsibility. We read, for example, "So, then each of us will give an account of ourselves to God" (Rom 14:12). Jesus also states, "But I tell you that everyone will have to give account on the Day of Judgment [for every empty word they have spoken]" (Matt 12:36). Revelation 22:12 adds to the emphasis stating that at the coming of Christ that God will "give to each person according to what they have done." Romans 2:6 concludes the emphasis, "When his righteous judgment will be reveal. God will give to each person according to what he [or she] has done."

The proposed interpretation of a two level approach to divine judgment not only takes into account the biblical emphasis on personal accountability, but also addresses the issue of children who die in infancy. While children may experience death as a *corporate* consequence of Adam's disobedience, they are not personally guilty before God having not personally or deliberately violated God's commands. Millard Erikson deduces a similar conclusion concerning the death of children in infancy when he writes,

> Despite having participated in that first sin, they [infants] are somehow accepted and saved. Although they have made no conscious choice of Christ's work [or of Adam's sin for that matter], the spiritual effects of the curse are negated in their case.[21]

Given the proposed two level interpretation of divine judgment, consider the author's concluding interpretation of imputed sin upon humankind. Briefly stated: Prior to the actual institution of law, sin was unspecified (since there was no law)

---

21. Erickson, *Christian Theology*, 638–39.

The Dysfunction of the Human Spirit

and consequently cannot be made the source of judicial judgment (Rom 5:13).[22] Nevertheless, *death* reigned and therefore judgment was imputed to all persons. Since the law did not at that time concretely exist, God viewed persons in Adam and hence all persons within the framework of a *trust-relationship* in God the Creator and God's Word. Henri Blocher places the emphasis for the imputation of original sin into the human experience on a violation of a supposed covenant *of creation*. But since the word *covenant* does not appear in the Genesis account of original sin, it is not evident that an actual *covenant* was established in Eden. Nevertheless, God did instruct our first ancestors of their responsibilities to care for creation and not to eat of the tree of the knowledge of good and evil. Did the command *not to eat of the tree*, then, constitute a covenantal-relationship which in turn instituted the necessity of obedience as a priority condition for continued relationship with God the Creator? Palmer Robertson believes that it did. Robertson writes,

> Radical obedience ... provides the key to blessing under the covenant of creation. If man will acknowledge fully the lordship of the Creator by obeying his word purely for the sake of obedience, he shall experience the consummate blessing of the covenant. Life in perpetuity shall be his.[23]

While the divine admonition regarding the tree obviously included the necessity of obedience, I believe the focus lies elsewhere. The admonition *not to eat of the tree* does not center first of all in a call to radical obedience for obedience sake, but is a summons for all humanity to *trust* God's guiding and protecting Word. The admonition focuses on a challenge of what I term *faith-obedience* (obedience emerging from within the context of a trust-faith relationship) in the goodness of God's protecting Word in contrast to what I term Robertson's *obedient-faith* interpretation (obedience constituting the basis of relationship with God). This

---

22. Blocher, *Original Sin*, 77.
23. Robertson, *Christ of the Covenants*, 83.

The Humanity of Christ

distinction, I believe, is critical to an interpretation of original sin and the command to be holy as God is holy.

That the original relationship between God and our first parents was a *faith-trust relationship*, not a *law-obedient based relationship*, is supported by the Genesis account. Since Adam-Eve originally did not possess either the knowledge or experience of sin nor did they possess an inherent propensity toward sin, no point of contact existed within human nature for initiating an attitude of *distrust* in God's Word of command and hence an act of disobedience. Thus, the goal of the first temptation centered on severing the *trust* relationship; that is, to entice the first humans to displace God as the sovereign Creator, by embracing an alternative word of promise; namely, "You will not surely die... When you eat of it, your eyes will be opened, and you will be like God, knowing good and evil" (Gen 3:4). If the human heart becomes sin's ally, humanity, then, will forever be under sin's dominion and its devastating consequence—separation from fellowship with God and the distortion of the capacity to be the persons God intended the human creatures to be. It will result in a reversal of the focus of the divine image, inverting the disposition of *trust* in God to one of *distrust*. It is this inversion of the spiritual core of human personhood grounded in the human spirit that grace must now overcome to produce a faith-relationship with God again.

In the absence of the law, judicial judgment cannot be imputed to persons since persons have no judicial culpability before God.[24] It is only with the coming of the law that individual judicial culpability is specifically ascribed. Nevertheless, Paul states that *death* (the consequence for sin—Rom 3:23) came upon those persons who did not sin as Adam did. But what constituted the basis for the judgment of death upon persons when there was no law?

I propose that divine judgment is found in the violation of the *faith-trust relationship* that God established with Adam in issuing the command *not to eat of the tree, a command* intended to reinforce the faith-trust relationship in the goodness of God and God's guiding Word. Even though those who did not sin as Adam

---

24. Blocher, *Original Sin*, 77.

The Dysfunction of the Human Spirit

did, they nevertheless sinned in some way. While their sin is not specifically stated, I propose that their sin was also a sin of rejecting the Lordship of God the Creator.[25] Like Adam, humanity's sin was a failure to trust and hence to honor and acknowledge God the Creator. Thus, those who did not sin like Adam (and Eve) who functions in both the New Testament and the Genesis creation account as archetypal beings of humanity and who also existed as real people in a real past,[26] also rejected God as the sole Creator, affirming their personal guilt before God by their idolatry. Sin, therefore, did not first constitute the breaking of a rule, but the breaking of a *trust/faith* relationship with God.[27] Their sin resided in the displacement of God as Creator, and in placing their trust in the potentials and objects of the created world, a reversal or the redirection of trust occurred. Note again the universal implications of the Apostle Paul's words,

> For although they [humankind] knew God, they neither glorified him as God nor gave thanks to him, but their thinking became futile and their foolish hearts were darkened. Although they claimed to be wise, they became fools and exchanged the glory of the immortal God for images made to look like a mortal human being and birds and animal and reptiles. (Rom 1:21-23)

That death came upon those who did not sin as Adam did, therefore, did not require that some legal standard of judgment had to exist from the time of Adam to Moses. What existed as a basis for judgment lay in the command concerning the tree, a command that focused on *trust* in the goodness of God the Creator.[28] Hence, the issue of the historical period from Adam to Moses, when there was no law, in which judgment was imputed to persons resides in the core basis of the command regarding the tree; namely, *trust* in God's lordship as Creator-God. The command concerning the tree, therefore, functioned in a similar manner to that of Adam's head-

25. Ibid.
26. Walton, *Lost World of Adam and Eve*, 96.
27. Mow, quoted in Bloesch, *Theological Notebook*, 1:46.
28. Blocher, *Original Sin*, 77.

The Humanity of Christ

ship; that is "it increased the efficacy of the reckoning of sin" and hence provides a key for interpreting the analogous roles between Christ and Adam in Romans 5.[29] The parallel between Christ and Adam serves as the grounding of the assurance that "the efficacy of Christ's role in justification and the fullness of life to come is as secure an inheritance as conversely Adam's disobedience incurred the certainty of condemnation and death for all."[30]

The focus of Romans 5:12–19, I propose, centers on *life and death*, on *condemnation and justification*. Blocher, I believe, points us in the right direction when he writes, "If Adam's role was so dramatically efficacious in securing the condemnation of all people in him, and therefore the reign of death, *how much more* [used four times (vv. 9, 10, 15, 17)] is Christ's work efficacious for those in him, leading to life eternal."[31] In other words, Adam functions as a type of Christ in the analogous manner that he is the source for the imputation of *death* as Christ is the source for the imputation of justification and *life*.[32]

Paul's teaching in Romans 5:12–19, therefore, focuses on the efficaciousness of the imputation of life and justification through Christ in the same manner in which death is imputed through Adam's disobedience. Since the notion of ontological corruption is absent in Paul's argument in Romans 5:12–19 (but may be inferred from the declaration in Romans 5:13 that all persons are constituted as sinners), it is, therefore, logical to deduce that the condemnation stressed by Paul finds its focus in the judgment of physical *death* as the concrete evidence of the loss of relationship with God and entails the separation from the life and purpose of God in creating humans and the world (Eph 4:18).

With the loss of relationship with God, the judgment of physical death simultaneously results in the dysfunction of the spiritual dimension of human personhood. Physical death brings

---

29. Blocher, *Original Sin*, 79.
30. Ibid.
31. Ibid., 80.
32. Ibid., 78.

The Dysfunction of the Human Spirit

decay and the increasing dysfunction of cognitive, physical, and spiritual capacities of human persons.

That the judgment of Adam's sin centers primarily on *death* can also be inferred from an interpretation of the grammatical construction ἐφ' ᾧ in Romans 5:12. The ἐφ' ᾧ παντα ἥρμαρτον ("because all have sinned") is a critical phrase and is often interpreted as *because* (all sinned), thereby stressing the *source* of sin's entrance into the human experience in Adam's act of disobedience. The pronoun ᾧ is, therefore, taken as a neuter pronoun implying Adam's disobedience as the cause of the imputation of sin upon humankind. On the other hand, ἐφ' ᾧ can be interpreted literally as meaning *upon whom* rather than *because* (though the translation of *because* cannot be totally ruled out), interpreting the relative pronoun ᾧ as a masculine pronoun, thereby making the ᾧ refer to its immediately preceding substantive *death* (*thanatos*) as the consequence of sin rather than the imputation of total corruption of the human self.[33] The Romans 5:12b text would, then read, *death came to all people* as the consequence of Adam's sin and because of death all people are constituted as sinners and separated from the life, love and care of God. This interpretation, I believe, offers a preferred approach to original sin and the Christian life in that sin has a natural source in death and the dysfunction of the human spirit rather than a general perspective in which the totality of human nature constituting the source of sin. If the dysfunctional human spirit could be healing and death defeated, Paul's emphasis on the freedom of the believer from the fear and power of death and the victory over the dictatorial power of sin becomes a realistic hope for every believer. The Apostle Paul writes, "For sin shall no longer be our master, because you are not under the law, but under grace" (Rom 6:14). Paul again declares on the basis of Christ's death and resurrection, "You have been set free from sin and have becomes slave to righteousness" (6:18). And finally in 6:22 Paul declares, "But now that you have been set free from sin and have become slaves of God, the benefit you reap leads to holiness and the result is eternal life." Paul is asserting that now that believers are united

---

33. Meyendorff, *Byzantine Theology*, 39.

The Humanity of Christ

with Christ's in his death and resurrection, believers are now free from the dictatorial power of sin, the law, and death and are there free To pursue a fuller, deeper intimate relationship with God.

Death, of course, entails more than simply the cessation of physical life. It also denotes a dysfunction at the spiritual core of creaturely life in that the human spirit has become separated from its essential ground and relationship with the Spirit of God. The sin of Adam, therefore, has imposed upon humanity not only a state of morality, death, and decay but also, and in an important sense for the thesis of the book, a radically distorted way of thinking and acting contrary to God's purpose in creating humans in the divine image.

While decay arises within human experience as well as within creation itself (Rom 8:20–21) as the consequence of the entrance of death, I contend that the consequence of the divine judgment finds its most critical impact in the dysfunction of the human spirit (the unique spiritual core of human self). This dysfunction creates a distorted way of seeing and thinking as a result of the loss of relationship with God. The spiritual dimension centering in the human spirit has been reversed, turning inwardly away from the care and need of one's neighbor and the acknowledgement of the Lordship of Christ to a dominant stress on self-interest and self-affirmation, jeopardizing any attempt to be holy as God is holy. It inverts the *exocentric* outlook of the human spirit away from its positive orientation to a negative one that promotes evil and perversity of all kinds.

If pressed to explain the dysfunction in terms of a *sinful nature*, I propose that it denotes a *dyslexic outlook* at the spiritual core of human existence. It denotes a structural distortion of the relational core of human existence that promotes injustice and evil of all kinds. To put it in an ethical context, the human spirit now possesses an orientation that places *trust* in the *value system* of this age; that is the *flesh*, a *value system* that stands opposed to divine direction in every imaginable way. Apart from divine grace, humankind is unable to grasp the significance of a way of life guided

The Dysfunction of the Human Spirit

by the value-system revealed in the cross—a value-system of self-sacrificial love for the sake of others.

To speak of a *sinful nature*, then, simply refers to a distorted way of seeing and thinking that manifests itself where self-interest comes in conflict with the needs of our neighbor, both individually and within the structural contexts of society and the inability to give honor and glory to God alone as the source of life. The *sinful nature*, if persuaded to use this phrase, simply denotes an *inauthentic* form of human existence.

To support the notion of the *sinful nature* by appealing to the Pauline concept of the *flesh* is not convincing. A major difficulty centers in the fact that Paul, contends Walter Russell, never uses the term *nature* (phusis) to denote life either in sin or in Christ, nor does Paul speak of persons possessing a sin nature.[34] Rather, when Paul uses the word *flesh* (sarx), he uses it in an extended sense to refer to fallen humanity's rejection (or indifference) to God both in terms of divine order and divine presence. Gordon Fee's explanation of Paul's use of flesh is helpful here.

> What began as a purely anthropological term in the physical sense evolved into an anthropological term in a more theological sense [from "creatureliness" to human frailty], and finally into Paul's unique usage in a thoroughly eschatological sense. For this reason . . . the translation *sinful nature* fails to convey Paul's meaning, since that tends to make it an anthropological term without adequately recognizing that for Paul it functions principally in an eschatological way.[35]

It is in this eschatological context that Paul contrasts the *flesh* with the *Spirit*. Here the terms denote two opposing *patterns of conduct*; that is, two different lifestyles or value systems. They denote respectively the *old* pattern of living independent of Christ while the Spirit refers to the *new* pattern of living inaugurated by the indwelling Spirit. D. S. Dockery, therefore, writes, "'Old person' and 'new person' are not ontological but relational in orientation. They

---

34. Russell, *Christian Perspectives on Being Human*, 208.
35. Fee, *God's Empowering Presence*, 818.

The Humanity of Christ

speak not of a change in nature, but of a change in relationship."[36] The *old person*, therefore, denotes that pattern of conduct that characterizes our life in Adam while the *new person* refers to the new pattern of living actualized in Christ and inaugurated in the life of the believer through the Spirit. Thus, to *walk in the Spirit* points to a pattern of conduct or value system exhibited in Christ and inaugurated in the life of believers by the indwelling Spirit. This new life is characterized by the manifestation of the virtues of patience, humility, kindness, generosity, compassion, etc.; that is, the new (eschatological) way of life inaugurated by death and resurrection of Christ. Believers, therefore, are admonished, urged, compelled, and motivated to conduct themselves according to this new pattern of life by the Holy Spirit. Conversely, to *live according to the flesh* does not denote a *sinful nature* but rather refers to a lifestyle that is lived for the gratification and/or fulfillment of creaturely appetites and selfish human ambitions that stand opposed to the way of the Spirit.

A potential example may be found not only when Paul writes to the Corinthians believers but also in Paul's description of the ethical traits of the flesh and the Spirit in Galatians 5:16–22. In 1 Corinthians 3:1–3 Paul addresses the believers, "Brothers, I could not address you as spiritual but as fleshly [worldly, NIV]—as mere infants in Christ... You are still fleshly [worldly]. For since there is jealousy and quarreling among you, are you not fleshly [worldly]?" Here Paul admonishes the Corinthian believers, not with reference to a sinful nature, but as *fleshly*, that is, with regard to their manner of conduct. The Corinthian believers are conducting their lives according to the *old* patterns of behavior (jealousy, quarreling, and behaving according to human inclinations) rather than living according to the new value-system inaugurated by the Spirit.[37] The spiritual tension experienced by believers, then, is not one of the *old nature*—the *sin nature*, in conflict with a *new nature* but of two diametrically contrasting patterns or value systems. This interpretation does not reject the notion that there exists a radical core of

---

36. Dockery, *Dictionary of Paul and His Letters*, 628.
37. Russell, "Apostle Paul's View," 223.

The Dysfunction of the Human Spirit

potential evil within human nature. It merely offers a more specific basis from which sin emerges in contradistinction to the sinful nature view that contains a more general perspective in which often implies that human nature in all its aspects is sinful.

Sin, of course, continues to impact human conduct as the result of the dysfunction (inversion) of the human spirit. With the loss of relationship with God, the human spirit has become divorced from its foundational ground in the divine Spirit and consequently, has become dysfunctional. By *dysfunction* is meant an *inversion* of the human spirit (the spiritual core of human personhood) that reverses its positive (open) orientation to love God and one's neighbor as oneself and the acknowledgement of God as the sovereign Lord and sole source of life to a negative (closed) orientation that affirms and cares for oneself before all others. This inward turn distorts the original *ecstatic* purpose of the human spirit into an *egocentric-outlook* that affects relationship both with God and others. Mary Grey, therefore, defined sin as "a deliberate blocking of the relational grain of human existence."[38] It is "the structural de-creation—the structural un-making of the world"[39] as God intended the world, as a community of persons, to function.[40] When the human spirit is separated from its relationship with God, it becomes, writes James Loder, "a self-contradictory dynamic without ground, meaning, or purpose in itself."[41] It becomes like "a troubled genius whose work astonishes us, but whose torment ends in self-destruction."[42]

As the unique capacity for engaging in self-relatedness that in scope and complexity exceeds that of our nearest fellow creatures, the human spirit functions as the *executive director* of the human person's self-relational capacity, intended to provide direction to the input of information received from creaturely capacities and one's environment. If, however, the human spirit becomes

---

38. Grey, *Falling into Freedom*, 241.
39. Ibid.
40. Ibid., 231.
41. Loder, *Logic of the Spirit*, 110.
42. Ibid.

The Humanity of Christ

inverted, the information received from our biological capacities and cultural environment becomes misdirected from its originally designed purpose to love God and one's neighbor as oneself.

If the unique essence of human personhood resides in the possession of a human *spirit*, and if the lost relationship with God entails the loss of the freedom to be the persons God created humans to be, human persons, then, cannot realize the personal self he/she was created to be apart from relationship with God. "I can only be myself," writes Stephen Evans, "by a relation to that ideal outside myself which has formed the self."[43] This assertion, of course, assumes that there is no normative ideal within human nature itself to realize what the created self is to be. But since human persons were originally created with the freedom to be or not to be in relation with God, humans, then, can choose to be or not to be in this formative relationship. However, human personhood is truly itself only as it participates in God and in the grace of God. Separated from its ground in God, the human spirit seeks that which it cannot in itself achieve; namely, the genuine self that God intended.

On the occasion of Adam's disobedience, humanity became dysfunctional at the core of its being at the level of its spiritual capacity, and humanity's natural gift of reason lost its ability to grasp the *significance* of God's truth unaided by divine Spirit and God's grace. By "significance" is meant that humanity is in a state of indifference to God's truth as the means for the restoration of humanity's dysfunctional-spiritual condition. This judgment, however, does not mean that God's gracious intention in creating the human creature has been set aside by sin. Sin does not constitute a break with God as the source of humanity's hope, for sin does not entail an absolute separation from the offer of divine grace. Sinfulness simply means that humanity has been released to live an existence that naturally turns away from God and as a consequence does not function in the manner in which it was created by God. The result is, to borrow Marjorie Hewitt Suchocki's phrase, *a*

---

43. Evans, *Kierkegaard's Christian Psychology*, 54.

The Dysfunction of the Human Spirit

fall into violence,[44] a rebellious misuse not only of creation but also of the purpose for which human creatures were created; namely, as persons-in community, existing for the care and benefit of one other.

To summarize the proposed interpretation of the dysfunction of the human spirit and its relationship to original sin, the following premises have been advanced.

First, humanity was created essentially good. No sin principle existed within the human creature coming forth from the divine creative act that precipitated a struggle between good and evil within the natural constitution of the human creature. God simply created the human person to think and to act in harmony with the nature God gave in the same sense that all creatures were created to function or act in agreement with the nature they possess by virtue of creation. Since the human creature originally did not possess the knowledge of evil, either experientially or conceptually, the deduction is, therefore, drawn that morality enters into the human situation as the consequence of sin, not as the initiator of sin.

Second, humans in distinction from nonhuman creatures were created with a capacity for *self-relatedness* that in depth and complexity of function far exceeds that of our nearest nonhuman creatures. This dimension of *self-relatedness* constitutes a positive orientation or *openness* that entails human *freedom*. Freedom here refers not only to the human capacity for self-transcendence, but also denotes a powerful drive reaching out in encounter with others in which its transforming force entails the freedom to be what humans were created to be. T. F. Torrance describes this openness as a *transcendental determination*[45] of human existence that constitutes the human creature as a human being before God in relation to other human beings. John Meyendorf, in commenting on the thought of Maximus the Confessor, states that humankind is truly

---

44. Suchocki, *Fall to Violence*.
45. Torrance, *Religion, Reason, and the Self*, 112.

The Humanity of Christ

itself only as it exists in relationship with God, expressed in relationship with other reciprocal beings.[46] This remarkable capacity for self-related encounters, I propose resides in the function of the human spirit. It is a function that enables humans to reflect the moral/spiritual character of God within the conditions of creaturely existence.

Third, sin emerges into the human experience as the consequence of a severed relationship with God due to humankinds' idolatrous rejection of God as the sovereign Creator. Its source is not from some innate deficiency within human nature,[47] but comes from a competitive word, an alternative promise in contradistinction to the divine command not to eat of the tree. The purpose of the origianl temptation was to create an attitude of *distrust* in the goodness of God's protecting and guiding command. If our first ancestors could be persuaded to distrust God's command, the trust-relationship with God would become severed and humankind would be separated from God's guiding and sustaining Word. The proposition is, therefore, held that the insertion of this alternative *word of promise; that is, you will not die*, created the context for the emergence of sin and initiated the temptation to abandon the faith-relationship with God.

Finally, the consequence of Adam's act of disobedience imputed to all Adam's descendants is a *corporate judgment* that imputes to humankind the certainty of physical death and the dysfunction of the human capacity to be the persons God created humans to be. Adam's sin introduced a distortion in the spiritual dimension of human existence that expresses itself in the inability to acknowledge God as Lord and the failure to care for one's neighbor before self-interest. We should take care, however, not to transfer the corporate unity of humankind into a radical individualism. At the same time, neither personal culpability nor personal salvation can be

---

46. Meyendorf, *Byzantine Theology*, 13.
47. Maximus the Confessor, *Photius Library*, 117.

The Dysfunction of the Human Spirit

realized in an individual's life without involving some notion of free choice.

God's judgment upon sinful humanity, however, is overwhelmed by God's grace. This unprecedented manifestation of grace finds its origin in the very nature of God, concretely expressed in God's Word of promise. The promise of God comes forth as a Word of hope, of rescue, of redemption, and of life itself. Upon the occasion of the first sin, there is immediately issued the promise of a *redeemer* (Gen 3:15), described as Immanuel, *God with us* (Isa 7:14), and identified as the *Mighty God* (Isa 9:6). Out of the love and graciousness of God's character the promise comes forth: a promise of reconciliation, of forgiveness (Ezek 36:24–25), and the possession of a new heart and a new spirit (Ezek 36:26).

While sin entails separation from God, it does not entail being separated from God's loving promise. In this promise lies humanity's only hope—a promise inseparably bound up with the person and work of Jesus Christ, whom God chose from the foundation of the world (Eph 1:4). As God's elected and anointed One, Christ becomes the promise of God through whom sinful humanity may become the adopted children of God (Eph 1:4). With divine certainty God is working out the divine purpose and plan which God predestined *in Christ* in accordance with the riches of divine grace (Eph 1:11, 7–8). It is a promise not only for the forgiveness of our sin, but also for the healing of the dysfunction of the human spirit—indeed, the healing of humanity itself. In Jesus Christ there is concretely exhibited the harmonious relationship between the divine Spirit and the human spirit that God intended to function within humanity created in the divine image. To be holy as God is holy, therefore, requires a healing of the human spirit so that redeemed persons may reflect in their daily conduct and in encounters with others the character of God revealed concretely in Jesus Christ.

4

The Healing of the Dysfunction of the Human Spirit

The glory of God is a human being who's fully alive

—IRENAEUS

The Spirit is the inner teacher by whose effort the promise of salvation penetrates into our minds, a promise that would otherwise only strike the air or beat upon our ears.

—JOHN CALVIN

THE DYSFUNCTION AND ITS CONSEQUENCES

Following the creation of the universe, God seems to pause. Something momentous is about to occur. The angels stand in wonder and unbelief as God announces, *Let us make humankind in our image, according to our likeness* (Gen 2:26). An unprecedented

The Healing of the Dysfunction of the Human Spirit

creature is about to be created and will be given a remarkable *gift*. This unprecedented *gift* resides in the creation of a creature that is declared to be in the *image* and *likeness* of God. The essence of the gift resides in the possession of a *human spirit*. This remarkable gift enables this creature to reflect the moral-spiritual character of God within their creaturely world, and is thus differentiates them from the other creatures. This unique creature has become identified as a *human* creature. The essence of this gift resides in the capacity to engage in *personal relatedness* that exceeds that of humankind's nearest creaturely relatives. It not only enables this creature to engage in personal relationship with other reciprocal creatures but also, and more importantly, to enter into fellowship (personal relationship) with the Creator. The core function of this unique capacity resides in the ability to love others in the same manner in which they love and care for themselves.

This gift also entails the capacity to *trust* God the Creator who cares for and sustains this uniquely created being. The necessity to maintain this *trust-relationship* between our first ancestors and God the Creator finds its rationale in the command *not to eat from the tree* of the knowledge of good and evil. The purpose of the command was to create a context for affirming the *trust-faith relationship* in the goodness of the Creator. Since a struggle between good and evil impulses did not yet exist for our first ancestors, their future remained in the loving purpose and care of the Creator. Life in perpetuity was theirs as the gift of God. It was life in all its fullness without conflict or tension between nature and grace, between the inner and outer dimensions of human personhood. As a gift of God, the life of our original ancestors functioned as a harmonious wholeness of being.

Something tragic, however, enters this idyllic scene. An alternative, competitive *word of promise* enters. It is a tempting word. It is a *word* challenging both God's goodness and the command of God's guiding and protecting word. The alternative word of promise, however, is based upon a lie; namely, *you will not die*. Hence the *promise* is a deceptive one because its purpose is to create doubt and thus unbelief in what God had said. The Tempter

The Humanity of Christ

assures our ancestors with an additional incentive, "You will be like God knowing good and evil." The deceptive purpose resides in the hope of severing the *trust-relationship* between God the Creator and our first ancestors. The temptation is powerful and enticing. The promise to possess the ability to discern between good and evil as God the Creator does, initiates a powerful temptation. But such a discerning capacity belongs exclusively to God and was not intended to be a task our original ancestors were created to bear.

Thus, the *word* of God that sustained our first ancestors in their relationship with God and hence the spiritual capacity to reflect the moral-spiritual character of God stands in jeopardy. To disobey God's guiding word will result not only in breaking of the trust-relationship with God but also entails the dysfunction of God's remarkable *gift* of the human spirit. The violation of God's command, therefore, entailed not only an act of disobedience but also constituted an act of breaking the heart of God. The displacement of God's lordship as Creator and the rejection of God's Word created a dysfunction in the relational capacity of the image of God in the human creature. Consequently, with the displacement of God, *trust* came to center in the alternative promise, resulting in the loss of fellowship with the divine source of human life and the consequence of a radical dysfunction in the core of human personhood. The spiritual capacity inherent within human spirit became misdirected and its originally divine purpose to love God and one's neighbor was radically reversed to focus predominately on the needs and desires of the human self.

When our original ancestors chose to displace God as the Creator, thereby reversing the worship of the divine Creator and adopting an idolatrous worship of the various creatures, humanity became separated from its essential foundation in God. This breach of *trust* resulted in humanity becoming separated from the life and loving care of God. Moreover, a dysfunction occurred within the human spirit that resulted not only in a broken relationship with the divine Spirit but also caused a reversal of the positive, *exocentric* orientation of the human spirit to a negative, *egocentric* outlook, resulting from a failure to *trust* God's guiding and

The Healing of the Dysfunction of the Human Spirit

sustaining word. Trust was transferred to creaturely potentials, and humankind came to regard themselves as autonomous beings independent of God. Humankind came to possess an inherent propensity to *trust* in the natural capacities of the human self and the supposed potentials of the newly created gods of nature—both of the earth and the sky. In our present worldly situation, trust and hope are placed in our technological advances and our scientific achievements. God is no longer a necessary component for grasping the meaning of life or an understanding reality.

This dysfunction at the core of human personhood is like a terrible disease that has penetrated the human psyche, distorting the human perception of the value and dignity of human life. While this dysfunction does not entail that humanity ceases to be human or that humanity is somehow creating a new creation by its misdeed,[1] it does mean that humanity has become "*inauthentic.*" By inauthentic is meant that humanity is not functioning—thinking or acting, in a manner that reflects the image of God in which humanity was originally created. Humanity has lost its humane (spiritual) rudder. This dysfunction (distortion), writes Ray Anderson, "is more than a sickness which can be cured by relieving persons from psychical and physical distress. It requires radical healing and restoration at the core of human personhood."[2] It requires the healing of the human spirit so that persons may function again according to the divine purpose for which they were originally created. Ellen Charry reflects on this tragic situation, "With its loss of relationship with God [and hence the divine Spirit], we [humans] do not really know who we are, from whence our life takes its orientation, or where we ought to direct our energies."[3] Charry continues the thought, "Without God we [humans] are liable to float aimlessly at the mercy of volatile emotions and hormones or be seduced by less worthy claims to deity. Or we may turn to a misguided search for fame, wealth, or power."[4]

1. Barth, *Church Dogmatics*, IV.1, 483.
2. Anderson, *On Being Human*, 99.
3. Charry, *By the Renewing of the Minds*, 3.
4. Ibid., 4.

The Humanity of Christ

While the human spirit impacts the physical, emotional, personal, and intellectual dimensions of human personhood, this dysfunction does not entail a total dysfunction of human personhood. Ray S. Anderson expressed the point this way:

> The removal of the *old nature* when a *new nature* is bestowed through regeneration of our humanity is not the taking away of our own humanity or personal identity, but the opening up again of our true self. It is like the restoration of sight to one blind from birth.[5]

While the human spirit is the source and motivation for the expression of *human spirituality*, it is not some mystical entity but is an intrinsic, pervading, influencing dimension within human nature that impacts and directs the attitudes and motivations of human personhood. It is, in fact, the substratum of our mental acts. It seems that there exists an inherent connection between the human spirit and the human mind.[6]

That a correlation exists between the human spirit and the human mind is offered merely as a reflection by one who has little background in neuroscience or neuropsychology. Having made the statement that the human spirit is the substratum of our mental acts is merely a deduction from my interpretation of the nature and function of the human spirit. This deduction, I believe, is coordinate with the *top-down* psychological viewpoint and is similar to the research of Roger Sperry on consciousness. Sperry writes,

> Consciousness is [often] conceived to be a dynamic emergent property of brain activity, [but actually is] neither identical with nor reducible to the neural events of which it is mainly composed . . . Consciousness exerts potent causal effects on the interplay of cerebral operation. In the position of top command at the highest levels in the hierarchy of brain organization, the subjective properties were seen to exert control over the bio physical and chemical activities at subordinate levels.

---

5. Anderson, *On Being Human*, 84.
6. Jeeves and Brown, *Neuroscience Psychology and Religion*, 28–29.

The Healing of the Dysfunction of the Human Spirit

Sperry summarizes,

> We do not [therefore] look for conscious awareness in the nerve cells of the brain, nor in the molecules or the atoms in the brain processing.[7]

I, therefore, suggest that the human spirit function within human nature in manner similar to the nature and function of human consciousness, but in a moral-spiritual context. In other words, when asked, what is consciousness we are in the same arena when we ask, what is the nature and function of the human spirit.

The dysfunction of the human spirit, I believe, has distorted the mind's perception of God's lordship as sovereign Creator of the world and God's revelatory truth graciously given to humankind. The rationale for this problem is the consequence of the rejection of God the Creator that resulted in the withdrawal of God's guiding and sustaining Word, allowing humanity to live under the authority of other masters, but also in the reversal of the human spirit's original purpose and function. God's judgment is described in the phrase, "God gave them [humankind] over" (Rom 1:24, 26, 28). Hence, the essence of God's judgment resulted in humanity's coming under the tyrannical lordship of sin and death—a lordship unworthy of humanity's trust and/or submission. It is a lordship incapable of exercising its reign in any but the most destructive ways—contrary to the divine purpose in creating humans to function in a manner that reflects in the divine image in which humans were created.[8]

While still possessing the capacity of personal freedom inherent in the human spirit, the human spirit, nevertheless, has turned in upon itself, deifying human autonomy, rejecting any acknowledgment of God as sovereign Lord and Creator, and thus embracing the belief that the ultimate meaning of human life resides in the pleasures and benefits that creaturely-intellectual potentials can provide. In theological terms, the essence of God's wrath upon humanity's idolatrous rejection of the Creator, and the consequent

---

7. Brown et al., *Whatever Happened to the Soul*, 88.
8. Achtemeier, *Romans*, 37.

The Humanity of Christ

dysfunction within human spirit, resides in God allowing humanity to have its own way; that is, allowing humanity to live in sin and in the consequence of its idolatrous rejection of God's bountiful love and care.[9] Humanity has lost its wholeness and integrity as spiritual persons, interpreting humanity principally in terms of its physical, emotional, and intellectual capacities. Nevertheless, humans have an almost unexplainable (inherent) desire to be and to act in a manner that constitutes some perceived standard of *right* conduct; that is, a desire to be what humans ought to be, yet seemingly unable to achieve. This *desire*, I propose, is initiated and motivated by the human spirit seeking its true function and home with the divine Spirit. Simply put, humans are like orphaned children lost in haunted woods without a genuine Father. Humanity can be characterized as being *ontologically alone*. Hence, due to the possession of the human spirit, humans experience an undefined spiritual *quest*, a search to be persons who embrace not only the *good* but also the purpose for which they exist in the world, yet failing to find a compelling or satisfying answer to this sense of *lostness* and a permanent or secure hope.

A REFLECTION ON THE NATURE OF THE RADICAL DYSFUNCTION: ONTOLOGICAL ALONENESS

In his instructive and challenging book *The Spiritual Quest: Transcendence in Myth, Science, and Religion*, Robert M. Torrance, as previous noted, describes this unexamined spiritual desire as a *quest*. Torrance writes that the quest is "pre-eminently a *conscious* transcendence, a deliberate reaching toward a posited—if by no means unalterable—goal, and in this purposeful overreaching of our given status, we are perhaps entitled to regard humankind, among the inhabitants of our planet, as being alone."[10] Professor Torrance further describes this quest as a "fundamental desire

---

9. Ibid., 40.
10. Torrance, *Spiritual Quest*, 3.

The Healing of the Dysfunction of the Human Spirit

to know precisely that for which it is searching." It embodies a spiritual search as the result of a lost relationship with God. Augustine expressed this notion as follows: "You have made us for yourself, O Lord, and our hearts are restless until it rests in you [God]."[11]

Robert Torrance comments on this spiritual quest as identifying us as *human* persons, stating that this spiritual quest "is the culminating expression of a universal activity by which humanity is in large part defined as human."[12] This *quest*, continues Torrance, "resides in a tension between closure and openness, *stasis* and change, collective ritual and individual aspiration."[13] It entails the "business of seeking, of setting off in determined pursuit of what we [humans] are lacking and may never attain, is no incidental theme of our literature and thought, no bypath of history, but, nevertheless, distinguishes humanity from lowlier beasts, designating humanity as *animal quaerens* with at least as much right as *animal rationale*."[14]

Albert C. Outler also reflects on the tragedy of human existence within the context of the *loss of the sacred*.[15] He traces the tragedy of modern society "to humankind's mortal illness to its ultimate cause in the almost total loss of the sense of the sacred with its consequent human disorientation from the moral order of God and its sometimes raging, sometimes apathetic, despair of meaning and value for human existence."[16] Outler further contends that "any serious consideration of *the loss* and recovery of the sacred plunges us straightway into the depths of our epoch's spiritual crisis. It carries us right down to our spiritual roots."[17] The dilemma of humanity can be expressed with the words: "Without Christ . . . without hope . . . without God." Outler summarizes humankind's

---

11. Augustine, *Basic Writings*, Volvol. 1, Book book Eight8.
12. Torrance, *Spiritual Quest*, xii.
13. Ibid., x.
14. Ibid., 3.
15. Outler, "Loss of the Sacred," 16.
16. Ibid.
17. Ibid.

The Humanity of Christ

tragedy with the premise, "Modern man has discovered that he who loses God loses not only hope but also his very humanity."[18]

Outler expresses the tragedy of the human situation from the words of Will Durant's notable book *The Story of Philosophy*. Durant writes,

> God who was once the consolation of our brief life and our refuge in bereavement and suffering has apparently vanished from the scene; no telescope, no microscope discovers him. Life has become in that total perspective which is philosophy, a fitful pullulation [swarm] of human insects on the earth; nothing is certain in it except defeat and death—a sleep from which, it seems, there is no awakening . . . It seems impossible any longer to believe in the permanent greatness of man, or to give life meaning that cannot be annulled by death.[19]

While possessing a sense of what humanity *ought* to be, yet seeing it only as a baffling image in a mirror, humanity, nevertheless, is unable to bring this vision of human wholeness to fruition due to the dysfunction of the human spirit. If a vision of wholeness or authentic humanity is to be realized, it will entail a decisive act of God, an act performed by the freedom of God's sovereign love and grace. Such a divine act will require overcoming the dictatorial power of sin and death and the fulfillment of the righteous requirements of the law under which humanity has been imprisoned (1 Cor 15:56). The law demands that humans conduct their lives in righteousness and holiness. With every misstep or violation humans make, the law's condemnation emerges, creating an awareness of guilt, shame, and hopelessness. The law closes the door to all attempts at achieving *authentic personhood* as God intended. This sense of condemnation constitutes the existential function or purpose of the law; namely, to intensify humankind's inability to meet the demands of righteousness and justice and thereby increasing an awareness of personal sins and acts of injustice as well as the inability of a religious, social, or political agendas to

18. Ibid.
19. Ibid.

The Healing of the Dysfunction of the Human Spirit

achieve an authentic humanity and/or spiritual and moral wholeness within human society.

If, however, the human spirit is healed of its dysfunction and humankind is to be restored, it will require a divine act that can only be likened to bringing into existence a *new creation* (a new person) and will entail a healing at the core of human personhood. This radical restoration will require God or a God equivalent *person*, who can fulfill on our behalf the righteous requirements of the law, a person whose righteousness and love can overcome the power of death for our sakes. Since the dysfunction exists within the realm of earthly existence, the healing will need to occur within the structures of earthly existence. In other words, the healing process will require this person equal in nature to God who chooses to become identified with us in our broken, distorted, and sinful condition in order to bring a healing to our dysfunctional human existence.

The underlying premise here is that the healing of the human spirit is intrinsically bound up in relationship with God. Since the uniqueness of human existence lies in the possession of the relational capacity enabled by the human spirit as an unprecedented gift of God, it is, then, through a restored relation with God through Christ that we are brought back to the wholeness and integrity of our human personhood. With the loss of relationship with God, humanity has become severed from its humanizing and personalizing ground in God.[20] Due to the dysfunction of the human spirit, humans lack the ability to become fully humane and caring persons that God created humans to be. The present dysfunction leads to perversity and selfish acts contrary to God's divine purpose in creating humans as unique within the created order of living beings. This restoration of the human spirit will require humankind to become *reconciled* with God and the *restoration* of the human spirit in order to accomplish this healing task.

---

20. Torrance, "Goodness and Dignity of Man," 317.

The Humanity of Christ

Regeneration: The Initial Component in the Healing of the Human Spirit

In an unprecedented act of grace and love, God, in the sovereign freedom of divine love, chose to redeem, to reconcile, and to restore humankind (and the world) by *reconciling* sinful persons back again into fellowship with the divine Trinitarian personhood of God through the life, death, and resurrection of Jesus Christ.

This healing process begins with the reversal of the human spirit's dysfunction through the *regenerating* work of the Holy Spirit. This regenerating experience is wrought in the core of human personhood by the Holy Spirit who creates a radical change in the dispositional-motivational core of human personhood in which the negative outlook that views one's own self as possessing unconditional significance is transformed into a positive perspective in which the regenerated person now grasps the importance of the command to love God and one's neighbor as one's self. The experience of regeneration entails not only the entrance of *new life* but also entails the transformational-healing of the human spirit. It involves a reversal of the human spirit's negative disposition of the rejection of God as God to a positive one in which the regenerated believer now grasps the meaning and significance of God's truth that before the regenerating experience, as John Calvin writes, *would only strike the air or beat upon our ears*.[21] The Apostle Paul concurs when he writes, "The person without the [regenerating work] of the Spirit does not accept the things that come from the Spirit of God but considers them foolishness, and cannot understand them because they are discerned only through the Spirit" (1 Cor 2:14).

The underlying premise here is that God's revelation in Jesus Christ has reconciliation and restoration as its goal. The Apostle Paul, therefore, writes, "For if, while we were God's enemies, we were reconciled to him though the death of his Son, how much more, having been reconciled, shall we be saved through his life" (Rom 5:10). Paul again writes, "Once you [humankind] were

---

21. Loder and Neidhardt, *Knight's Move*, 19.

The Healing of the Dysfunction of the Human Spirit

alienated from God and were enemies in your minds because of your evil behavior. But now he [God] has reconciled you by Christ's physical body to present you holy in his sight, without blemish and free from accusation" (Col 1:21–22). The enmity between God and humankind has been removed and a permanent status of peace now exists (Eph 2:14). The Apostle Paul, therefore, writes, "But now in Christ Jesus you who once were far away have been brought near through the blood of Christ. For he himself [Christ] is our peace" (Eph 2:13–14). Again Paul writes, "For if, when we were God's enemies, we were reconciled to him though the death of his Son . . . we also rejoice in God through our Lord Jesus Christ, through whom we have now received reconciliation" (Rom 5:10–11). The ground of this new life and friendship, then, resides eternally in the death and resurrection of Christ. We have a comrade, a friend, a defender in Jesus Christ who always lives to intercede on our behalf as a permanent High Priest (Heb 7:18–28).

Acknowledging the dysfunction of the human spirit as a negative spiritual disposition that rejects God as God also entails the conclusion that humankind lacks the spiritual resources or potentials within human nature to overcome this distortion at the core of human personhood; that is, to reverse the human spirit's dysfunction in order to initiate *trust* again in God. If *trust* in God is to be reborn within humankind, God will need to take the initiative. This initiative will be inaugurated, not as a consequence of some eternal necessity within the nature of God, but as a consequence of the power and sovereign freedom of love that God is.

If sinful human persons are to be restored into fellowship with a righteous and holy God, a radical renewal needs to occur. Within Protestant evangelical theology, this divine restoration is referred to as *regeneration*. Regeneration (paliggensia) denotes the experience of being made alive again, or in traditional language, *born-again*. This biblical teaching of regeneration denotes the implanting of *new life* within the believer that entails the restoration of the moral-spiritual disposition in which the governing disposition of sinful persons becomes positively oriented so as to trust in God and to love one's neighbor. The *efficient cause* of this

The Humanity of Christ

regeneration resides in the transforming work of the Holy Spirit. It denotes an instantaneous change in the governing disposition of the believer that creates the desire to know, love, worship and serve God. The biblical basis for this change lies grounded in the believer's union with Christ by faith in his death and resurrection. The consequence of this experience is that believers are rescued from the dominion of darkness and placed into the kingdom of God's Son; that is, under the care, love, and authority of Christ in whom believers have redemption, the forgiveness of sins (Col 1:13–14). This transformation takes place as the Holy Spirit comes to indwell the believer upon repentance and faith in Christ. The believer now belongs to Christ, is adopted into the family of God, and is sealed by the Holy Spirit (2 Cor 1:21–22; Eph 1:13–14).

The Human Spirit and the Healing Power of Divine Love

The motivating and directing force of all God's actions are grounded in the freedom of God's sovereign love. Professor T. F. Torrance expresses the freedom and power of God's love clearly when he writes,

> God creates not out of necessity but purely in the freedom of love that God is; it is out of this intrinsic fellowship of personal being and love that God wills not to exist for the divine Self alone and brings a world into existence, forms human beings out of the dust of the earth, and gives them an integrity of their own out of sheer grace and love so that God may share His communion of love and personal being with them.[22]

Professor T. F. Torrance then concludes with the premise,

> The ultimate rational ground of the universe and the restoration of humankind [resides] in the beneficent nature and love of God.[23]

---

22. Torrance, *Trinitarian Faith*, 90–91.
23. Ibid., 93.

The Healing of the Dysfunction of the Human Spirit

Elmer Colyer offers an insightful exposition of Professor Torrance's interpretation of God's love as follows, "The why of the world and God's redemptive acts of restoration is the ungrudging goodness [and love] of the triune God."[24]

Professor T. F. Torrance cautions us about adopting an incorrect interpretation of the power of divine Love. Professor Torrance writes, "We should not think of the power of God's love in the abstract manner of pure unlimited power . . . Rather, the Creator's sovereignty is the living power of God the Father that flows from God's inmost nature and life as the movement of love that God is as Father, Son and Holy Spirit."[25]

The Apostle John straightforwardly declares, "God is love" (1 John 4:8). Adrio Konig reflects on this indispensable Christian declaration, and states, to say that "God is love is not simply to offer a theoretical designation of God, but is rather a conclusion to be drawn from the whole of salvation-history"[26] The biblical God is a God who *acts*, who makes himself known through his deeds, evidenced throughout the history of God's interaction with his people (deliverance from Egypt, life in Canaan, the Exile and Return). Professor Konig continues, "It is the God of love who is acting; the God who, unlike the gods surrounding Israel, who cares for his people, loves his creation and is prepared to make the highest sacrifice to give himself for the need and the preservation of humanity."[27] T. F. Torrance again provides insight into the nature of God's love, "We do not think of God as the eternal Being who also loves . . . but of God as a Being who is love."[28] The love of God, writes Adrio Konig, "is a love that goes out to a worthless object, giving it value. God does not love the world (and humankind) in the sense that he desires something that he does not have and can only get from humans. God's love for the world and humankind is a love that gives; a love that enriches the lives of humankind and

---

24. Colyer, *How to Read Torrance*, 161.
25. Ibid.
26. Konig, *Here Am I*, 38.
27. Ibid.
28. Torrance, *Christian Doctrine*, 148.

only in this way enriches his own."[29] Professor Adrio Konig, therefore, concludes, "To assert that God is love is the deepest meaning of the doctrine of Christ's divinity."[30]

God's love, therefore, drastically differs from the view of love found, for example, in the early Greek philosophers, such as Plato, in which love was understood as the desire for something that has value. Here the use of the word *eros* dominates. Leon Morris notes that the word *eros* refers to the love of the worthy, a love that desires to possess something that is worth possessing.[31] The biblical view of love, on the other hand, entails an act that gives values to those often viewed as worthless or unworthy of love. Thus, if love is the motivating and directing force of all God's actions and purposes, it cannot, then, be limited in its expression. For if love by its inherent nature includes freedom, the deduction, then, is that it is not conditioned by any outside influence other than divine love itself. This means that God is free to create, sustain, reconcile and restore creation and humankind, and that God does this on the basis of divine love both for creation and its creatures without partiality.[32]

The Incarnation and the Healing of the Human Spirit

It is in the self-giving and sacrificial act of God in Jesus Christ in the incarnation that we come not only to know the transforming power of God's love by which the human spirit experiences the healing (transformational) power of the renewal of life through the work of the Holy Spirit, grounded in the redemptive work of Christ. The author to the Epistle to the Hebrews, therefore, informs us of the divine act of God in the incarnation when he writes,

---

29. Konig, *Here Am I*, 37.
30. Ibid., 338.
31. Morris, *Testaments of Love*, 338.
32. Anderson, *On Being Human*, 163.

The Healing of the Dysfunction of the Human Spirit

> When Christ came into the world, he said, "Sacrifice and offering you did not desire, but a *body* you prepared for me; with burnt offerings and sin offering you were not pleased, Then I [Christ], said, 'Here I am—it is written about me in the scroll—I have come to do your will, my God.'" (Heb 10:5–7)

By means of the incarnation Christ, the Son of God, became one with humanity. He adopted our alienated and broken human nature in the incarnation in order that he may free us from the penalty of sin. Elmer Colyer offers insight into T. F. Torrance's view that is instructive. Colyer writes,

> Through the incarnation the actual root of our alienation in the ontological depths of our corrupt and fallen humanity, Christ has set us free from the power of sin and its companion—death.[33]

It is important to note here that in the incarnation Jesus not only became one with humankind in our brokenness and alienation from God, but also in assuming human existence, Christ through the hypostatic union restored a *faith-trust* component into the human situation that was originally broken by our first ancestors. It is profitable, I believe, at this point to note that in his human identity with us Jesus fulfilled all the righteous requirements essential for restoring a relationship with holy and sovereign God. The Apostle Paul writes, "Through the incarnation Christ by the power of the Spirit condemned sin in the flesh in order that the righteous requirement of the law might be fully met in us" (Rom 8:3b–4). It is important to note here that in Paul's phrase "the righteous requirement of the law," the word "requirement" is singular. So what, then, is this one righteous requirement? I suggest that Jesus in his assigned task as the *agent of redemption* restored the faith-trust dimension back again into human existence not only by his faithfulness to the task to which God assign him but also as sacrifice of atonement for our sins (Rom 3:25).

---

33. Colyer, *How to Read Torrance*, 88.

The Humanity of Christ

In other words, Jesus embraced the purpose of God and trusted that his life and death would accomplish the redemption and restoration of human persons that God appointed him to do. The Apostle Paul, therefore, writes, "God presented [appointed] Christ as a sacrifice of atonement, through the shedding of his blood—to be received by faith" (Rom 3:25). The words of Jesus, cited prior to his crucifixion, namely, *your will be done*, cited in Hebrews 7 and then again at Gethsemane, express Jesus' faith and submission to the purpose (will) of God to present himself as an atoning sacrifice on our behalf. The word translated *presented* in Romans 3:25 contains the meaning of *appointed* (προέθετο), in this case as the divine agent of redemption. The *Greek-English Lexicon of the New Testament* offers the following meaning of προέθετο: "to set before someone as a task/duty."[34] Jesus, therefore, undertakes both the redemptive task assigned to him by the Father, but also inserts into human experience the element of genuine faith and gratitude offered to God as a genuine human on behalf of humankind.

The event of the incarnation, therefore, is not merely an external event, that is, simply the cancellation of the judgment of God for our sin, but is also a very *personal event*; that is, Christ identified with us in our dysfunctional and alienated humanity by invading the tyranny of sin and judgment and death so that we might be set free for fellowship with God the Father through the atoning work of Christ and receive the gift of the Holy Spirit. I believe that T. F. Torrance conveys the meaning, purpose, and function of the incarnational-atoning work of Christ in a way that is theologically insightful:

> Through the incarnation the atonement is established and anchored in our human existence but also in the transcendent being and love of God from whom it derives and by whom it restores us in the communion of God's reconciling [and restorative] love.[35]

---

34. Danker, *Greek-English Lexicon*, 889.
35. Torrance, *Mediation of Christ*, 65.

The Healing of the Dysfunction of the Human Spirit

It is, therefore, through Christ's complete identification with us in our estranged and dysfunctional humanity, acting on our behalf, for our sakes, and in our place that the incarnate Son of God restores us in our alienated human spirit as those who have become separated from the life of God. In essence, through the atoning work of Christ in the incarnation, Christ sanctifies human nature in and through himself. Christ becomes the *vicarious human* for us all.[36] To be a *vicar* refers to someone who stands in the place of another or who stand as a representative for others. Through his death and in the incarnation, Christ becomes a sacrifice of atonement on our behalf. By accepting and embracing the will of God for our sake, Christ overcomes human alienation and guilt through his atoning work for our sake. While sanctifying human nature in himself, on our behalf, and by becoming united with us in our humanity, Christ inaugurated a *new humanity* open to those who become united with him by faith.[37] If newness of life is to be the experience of humankind, Christ must defeat sin, overcome sin's cohort, the law, and its ally, death. An *atoning exchange* takes place within the depth of our distorted, broken, and rebellious humanity by Christ's penetrating into those depths in the hypostatic union of the divine and human natures.[38] This *atoning exchange* is admittedly a great mystery. The redeeming act of God through the incarnation and death of Christ "is an unfathomable mystery before which the angels veil their faces and into which we cannot fully unfold but before which our minds bow in wonder, worship and praise."[39]

No contemporary theologian, in my opinion, has better expressed the significance of the incarnation and its impact upon the redemption of humankind than Thomas F. Torrance, and his most competent interpreter, Elmer M. Colyer. Colyer explains Torrance's viewpoint:

---

36. Ibid., 24–25.
37. Ibid., 65.
38. Torrance, *Mediation of Christ*, 64–65.
39. Torrance, *Karl Barth*, 239.

The Humanity of Christ

Jesus Christ embodies the reality of salvation in his divine-human reality. Christ does not mediate an atoning reconciliation other than what he is. He is in his own incarnate person the reality and content of the atoning redemption that he mediates.[40]

Christ's atoning work, of course, is also intimately connected with the resurrection. All that Christ achieved through his incarnational union with humanity would be incomplete apart from the resurrection. The Apostle Paul states that God's judgment for sin is *death* (Rom 3:23; 5:12–15).

In the event of the resurrection, God triumphs over *death* and brings into existence an entirely new *reality*—a reality not subject to the power and fear of physical death. The resurrection constitutes an event that stands on the same plane as the creation of the universe. In the resurrection, Christ defeats death for us. Death is an enemy that distorts and decays human capacities especially that of the human spirit, and provides the concrete evidence that humanity is separated from the life of God.

Separated from the divine Spirit, the human spirit is radically distorted and dysfunctional. On the other hand, restored or reconciled to God, the human spirit is enabled to function again as God intended. Death, of course, constitutes an inescapable condition of human existence. Even the most secular human person comes up against an impenetrable barrier when confronted with the reality of human death. It is an experience that ought not to be but is. Death constitutes the concrete, visible reality of both God's judgment upon humanity and the evidence of sin within human existence.

The entrance of *new life* into the world through the resurrection of Christ, therefore, stands in contrast to the temporal-spacial reality of our worldly-human dimension of life. Only in the primal miracle of the resurrection does God bring forth *new life*. If God is the fountain of all life, then God alone controls the reality of life which he causes to break forth in the primal act of the resurrection of Christ. As the sovereign act of God in creating the world *creato*

---

40. Colyer, *How to Read Torrance*, 89.

The Healing of the Dysfunction of the Human Spirit

ex nihilo, so in an analogous sense, the intervention of God in the resurrection produces something radically *new*. God's sovereign creative power brings forth life from the dead. The miracle of the resurrection, compared to the creation of the world, is the second and decisive action of the fullness of life and power that is in God. The resurrection produces a *reality* upon which all life depends. As Walter Kunneth, writes, "The pseudo life of the immanent world can only be a likeness as a symbol of the genuine life of the resurrection."[41]

This book, therefore, advocates the following interpretative premise; namely, that the Christian life and redemption should not be exclusively interpreted from within the context of *law* in which a forensic doctrine of justification takes priority over a fuller understanding of salvation (though justification is the foundation by which God can declare sinners as his children), but from the paradigm of newness of *life*. The paradigm of *life*, I believe, is a more promising approach in grasping the core of God's purpose in redemption. Through the incarnation, "we can no longer think of God as immutable and impassible—as a God who is remote and unknowable but rather as intensely personal and dynamic."[42] Colyer expresses Torrance's point this way, "Incarnational redemption unites the personal and the ontological within the incarnational reality of Jesus Christ as mediator. Atoning reconciliation takes place within the personal life and being of Jesus Christ."[43] By assuming oneness with us, Christ heals our diseased, alienated, dysfunctional humanity not only by Christ's being condemned on our behalf, but also reconciling and redeeming us so that we may participate in union and communion with the triune life of God though Christ in the Holy Spirit who unites us with Christ.

41. Kunneth, *Theology of the Resurrection*, 73.
42. Torrance, *Trinitarian Faith*, 156.
43. Colyer, *How to Read Torrance*, 89.

The Humanity of Christ

Spirit as the Agent of transformational Change

The initial experience of the healing of the human spirit is forgiveness. As Ray Anderson contends that in the message of Jesus there is a correlation of forgiveness and healing. Anderson writes, "Forgiveness is a praxis of the Spirit of Christ wherein we are set free from the self-accusation and shame that results from our alienation from God as the source of life."[44] To be forgiven entails an understanding of the meaning of renewal. Anderson continues the thought, "The word of [forgiveness] from sin based on the work of Christ in salvation history is premature apart from the praxis of forgiveness as the work of Christ in the hearts and lives of people through the empowering presence of the Holy Spirit."[45] It is the sovereign power of divine grace that forms the foundation of our concept of the recovery of authentic personhood. This recovery or renewal involves the specific work of the Holy Spirit that I identify as the divine *agent* of spiritual change. To interpret this change as *spiritual transformation* should not be taken to imply that spiritual change is the only change that occurs. Since humans exist as body and soul as well as possessing a human spirit, the renewal will by association affect the wholeness of human personhood. The Holy Spirit as the *divine agent of change* transforms the human spirit, enabling the human spirit to respond positively to God's truth and to be changed motivationally and dispositionally at the core of human personhood so we (believers) may now begin to love, obey, worship and acknowledge God as the foundation of life and goodness. To be *renewed by the spirit*—to borrow a phrase from the Apostle Paul (Rom 12:2), denotes having *the mind of Christ* (Phil 2:15). This transformation of the mind is the specific work of the Holy Spirit who engages the human spirit who, then, submits to the truth penetrated into the mind of believers through the work of the Holy Spirit. In the analogous manner that the Holy Spirit guided and empowered Jesus during his earthly sojourn through the hypostatic union of the two natures in his one person of Jesus,

---

44. Anderson, *Ministry on the Fireline*, 60.
45. Ibid., 66.

The Healing of the Dysfunction of the Human Spirit

so believers, in conducting their human life, are to be guided and empowered by the indwelling Holy Spirit. Thus, to be renewed by the Spirit is in essence to possess the *mindset of Christ* (Phil 2:5). John Wesley offers helpful insight when he contends that the *mindset* of Christ denotes a person who is indwelt and overpowered with the love of Christ. Christ reveals that God is not merely a divine being who happens to practice loving acts but is in his very being love itself. The believer who would strive to be *perfect*, contends Wesley, is a believer who practices love on all occasions and in all situations as Christ did. Wesley writes,

> [The believer who is mature in Christ] is one in whom is the mind which was in Christ . . . It is to be a believer whose heart is so all-flame with the love of God as continually to offer up every thought, word, and work, as a spiritual sacrifice, acceptable to God through Christ. To have the mind of Christ through the indwelling of the Spirit is neither more nor less than pure love—love expelling sin and governing both the heart and life. It is love excluding sin; love filling the heart, taking up the whole capacity of the soul . . . For as long as love takes up the whole heart, what room is there for sin therein?[46]

As the *divine agent of change*, the Holy Spirit is the embodiment of the life and empowering presence of God. It is in this context that the notion of *power* in association with the ministry of the Holy Spirit the issue of interpreting the Spirit's power arises. When we contemplated the *power* of the divine Spirit, we must be careful to avoid employing concepts of abstract notions of power drawn from our earthly experiences and observation. T. F. Torrance offers solid counsel when he reflects on the notion of the *power* of the Holy Spirit, God or Christ. Torrance writes,

> God's omnipotence, as revealed in Jesus Christ, actually conflicts with concepts of unlimited arbitrary power that humanity often constructs on the basis of worldly experience, absolutizes, and then attributes to God.[47]

46. Dayton, "Entire Sanctification," 523.
47. Torrance, *Trinitarian Faith*, 204.

The Humanity of Christ

Torrance continues,

> We must reject all abstract notions of divine omnipotence, for omnipotence is not to be understood in terms of what we think God can do, defining it as potency raised to the nth power, i.e., as omni-potence, but in terms of what God actually is and actually has done . . . every abstract question about what God can and cannot do and any discussion of God's power apart from who God is as Father revealed in Jesus Christ the Son is an empty movement of thought.[48]

Holy Scripture clearly identifies the manifestation of divine power with the work of the Holy Spirit. In Acts 1:8, for example, Luke declares, "You shall receive power when the Holy Spirit comes upon you." To convey the notion of the Spirit's power Luke uses the Greek word *dynamis*. This word may be defined as (1) the manifestation of awesome force, strength, or power; such as, the supernatural manifestation of God's power exhibited in miracles, signs, and wonders. Or (2) as the ability or capability to produce remarkable change. While other words are also used in the New Testament to convey the notion of power, the word *dynamis* dominates when referring to the power of the Holy Spirit. Bernard Loomer offers an explanation of the notion of *power* that I find helpful and instructive. Loomer suggests two uses of power; namely, (1) unilateral power and (2) relational power[49] that are applicable in interpreting the Spirit's power. Consider the first use noted by Loomer; namely, *unilateral power*.

Unilateral power denotes the capacity to control, influence, or force change by virtue of authoritative status alone. This type of power is evidenced everywhere in the concourse of daily life. We can observe it in governments, corporations, political dictatorship, war, etc. It is the power to affect change in others or even to act for someone's benefit (happiness, wealth, pleasure, or simply as an expression of authoritative position); that is, to impose one's viewpoint or will upon others. Unilateral power conveys a notion

---

48. Torrance, *Christian Doctrine*, 204.
49. Loomer, *Process Studies*, 5–32.

The Healing of the Dysfunction of the Human Spirit

of power that brings about immediate and drastic change as a consequence of overwhelming force, authority, or might. As such, unilateral power always proceeds from a position of strength. Consider the last time you were stopped by a police officer for supposed speeding. You may argue with the officer, but in the end he will win and you will have a ticket. Unilateral power functions within a hierarchical structure because it possesses the power or authority from the top, i.e., from the highest authority in a given situation. Negatively, unilateral power can be selfish and destructive; but it can also be positive—that is, it can be exercised for the benefit of others.

Unilateral power can be observed in Holy Scripture. It denotes the power of God manifest in miracles (Luke 5:17), in dealing with principalities and powers (Eph 6:10–18; 4:27), and in the triumph over evil (1 Cor 15:24–26). In these contexts, power is manifested as overwhelming authority or force from above. While unilateral power belongs to God, it is always used in a positive and beneficial manner in line with God's divine purpose. Consequently, Scripture speaks of unilateral power as *God's power, the power of the Kingdom of God*, and as *the power of Christ's death and resurrection*. The New Testament also identifies this *power with the gospel*; that is, the power of God unto salvation (Rom 1:16–17). As a manifestation of unilateral power, God's power is used positively, that is, to actualize God's good will and loving purposes for all living things.

Because unilateral power is subject to misuse, Scripture warns believers about its mesmerizing effects, tempting us to identify this power with ourselves and the glory it manifests. This was the case with Simon who sought to purchase the power of the Holy Spirit with money (Acts 8:18–19) and thus had no part in its possession or manifestation (Acts 1:21). In the history of the Christian church, as well as in Holy Scripture, persons who were agents of the manifestation of God's power were always careful to remain in the background and give the glory to God alone. These persons took great care not to touch that which belongs rightfully to God. They viewed themselves as servants and not as indispensable

The Humanity of Christ

ministers of that power. Consequently, unilateral power possesses the danger associated with authoritative power derived from position in hierarchical structures and from the desire for the possession of power for power's sake. Unilateral power, therefore, can alienate and isolate people by regarding them as objects for the demonstration of power or, conversely as obstacles to the manifestation of power.

Unilateral power finds its most compelling illustrations in our selfish, sinful world. Here unilateral power abounds. As Christians, we must, therefore, take great care that we do not desire to see the manifestation of God's power so that we can become objects of its glory. We must also guard against wanting to exercise power in a competitive manner in order to show that our power of achievement is greater than that of others. It is because of this inherent danger that Scripture points us to another kind of power, a marvelous power, a gentle power, which we often dismiss in the same manner that the world dismisses the power revealed in the apparent weakness of the cross. I classify this notion of power as *relational power*.

Relational power is not the power that forces change simply by virtue of its power to do so. Relational power is the power to move others to change. It is the power of relationship, characterized by openness, vulnerability, and a willingness to suffer on behalf of others. This notion of power, I believe, fits more naturally and consistently with the work of the Spirit whom I identify as the *Agent of Change*. As the Agent of Change, the Holy Spirit changes believers motivationally and dispositionally at the core of their human personhood (human spirit) so that the desires and attitudes of Christ exhibited in his incarnate life are reproduced in them. Change here is set in the *paradigm of life* and is conveyed through the metaphor of birth and personal growth and the transformation of the mind (Rom 12:2). With regard to the understanding of the notion of *power*, the motto of believers should be: *The power of love, not the love of power*. The work of the Holy Spirit is to transform the way we think and act by producing in us those character traits which mark the life of Christ is us. This view of power implies

The Healing of the Dysfunction of the Human Spirit

that godliness does not reside first and foremost in the manifestation of unilateral power but in the supernatural demonstration of a life marked by tender-heartedness, gentleness, patience, long-suffering, self-control, meekness, humility, joy, peace, and love. Paul referred to this as the manifestation of the *fruit of the Spirit* in believers. Ellen T. Charry expressed the point this way:

> Paul appreciated the renewing of the mind, which was necessary for Christian formation, required decisive action, symbolic rites and practices in which believers can profess their new identity, and commitments.[50]

Professor Charry continues her thought,

> Participation or union with Christ through the work of the Holy Spirit is the act by which believers are consecrated to Christ and absorb his power. Paul, of course, uses a multitude of images to capture the drama of the event: *newness of life, new creation,* or a *new self* (Rom 6:4; Cor 5:17; Gal 6:14–15; cf. Col 3:9–10); becoming or *being formed, conformed, created, or indwelt by Christ or the Holy Spirit, or transformed into the image of Christ* (Rom 8:9–11, 29–30; 1 Cor 6:19–20; 2 Cor 3:18; 6:16b–17; Gal 2:20; 4:19; Phil 3:21; cf. Eph 2:10; 3:17); [and] putting on or being clothed with Christ.[51]

The Significance of the Healing of the Human Spirit

The healing of the human spirit occurs when the divine Spirit confronts the human spirit with the truth of redemption revealed in the life, death, and resurrection of Jesus Christ. Confronted with the truth of absolute forgiveness and newness of life, the human spirit submits to the divine truth, and accepts by faith Jesus Christ as the Lord, Savior, and Guide of his/her life. Apart from

---

50. Charry, *By the Renewing of your Minds*, 4.
51. Ibid., 44.

The Humanity of Christ

the convicting and impacting work of the Holy Spirit, relationship with Christ does not occur, as John Calvin writes,

> The Spirit is the inner teacher by whose effort the promise of salvation penetrates into our minds, a promise that would otherwise only strike the air or beat upon our ears.[52]

Through submission and trust in God through the work of the Holy Spirit, the human spirit's radical dysfunction is transformed and restored back into its relationship with the divine Spirit of God. Believers now possess a spiritual openness and orientation toward the source of life itself; namely, the divine Spirit. This initial convicting work of the divine Spirit and the human spirit's submission is what constitutes the theological-biblical concept of *conversion*. For the human spirit separated from its foundation in the divine Spirit is like a ship without a sail that flows aimlessly by whatever current is strongest at the time. But healed through relationship with God, the human spirit becomes an image of the moral-spiritual character of God at the creaturely level, as James Loder put it, *a human figure for the divine reality*.[53] Loder explains, it is the

> Divine Spirit alone [that] can set the human spirit free from its proclivity to self-inflation, self-doubt, self-absorption, and self-destruction, and free for its magnificent obsession to participate in the Spirit of God and to know the mind of God [revealed in the person of Jesus Christ].[54]

To conclude, the basic interpretative premise undergirding the thesis of the book: namely, God created human persons as unique within the order of created creatures so that by divine grace and our continued response to that grace we might be restored back to the *image of God* in which we were originally created and for the purpose for which we were created. This premise entails

---

52. Calvin, *Institutes*, 541.
53. Loder and Neidhardt, *Knight's Move*, 48.
54. Loder, *Logic of the Spirit*, 10.

The Healing of the Dysfunction of the Human Spirit

that salvation not only includes absolute forgiveness of sin but also constitutes the act of God's unprecedented gift of grace and love. Here the emphasis on the healing of the human spirit centers on the restoration and maturing of the spiritual life. God has committed the divine resources to restoring human persons; indeed, creation itself, back again to function according to the purpose in which God originally created them and as such constitutes the ultimate goal of redemption. This goal, of course, required the defeat of sin, Satan, death, the fulfillment of the law, and the overcoming of evil as well as the restoration of the natural order of creation. God will have his creation and those creatures created in the divine image *whole* again. God will not permit Satan, evil, and moral disorder to have immortality. God will bring all things back to their originally designed wholeness at the consummation of all things. The Apostle Paul reflects on this glorious consummation:

> For creation waits in eager expectation for the children of God to be revealed. For the creation was subjected to frustration, not by its own choice, but by the will of the one who subjected it, in hope that the creation itself will be liberated from its bondage to decay and brought into the freedom and glory of the children of God. (Rom 8:19–21)

With the healing of the human spirit, the process of restoration begins. Jesus refers to this healing experience with the biological metaphor of *growth*. I propose introducing the term *salvationizing* to convey the developmental-transforming process by which God through the Holy Spirit on the basis of Christ's atoning sacrifice enables believers to grow into Christ-likeness. The Holy Spirit produces in the lives of believers what Paul designates as the *first-fruit of the Spirit*; that is, the manifestation of those virtues or character traits that mark the life of the Spirit within, the creation of a new spiritual disposition through the indwelling of the Holy Spirit at the time believers are united with Christ by faith.

5

The Fruit of the Spirit
The Ultimate Goal of the Holy Spirit's Restoration

IF THE POWER OF the Holy Spirit predominately centers in relational power, and if relational power finds expression in Christ-like character traits, it is logical, then, to identify spiritual maturity with the manifestation of Christ-like character traits or virtues. For being a Christian in the New Testament in any deep sense means to bear the fruit of the Holy Spirit[1] and the fruit of the Spirit is essentially character traits which manifest the life of God's Spirit within us. Thus "to possess the fruit of the Spirit is not really to possess something in the ordinary sense," writes Professor Robert C. Roberts, "but to be something."[2] It is to bear in one's person the imprint of the Spirit of God.

"Whatever else Christianity may be understood to be," declares Robert C. Roberts, it is a way of living and responding to others and to our world. "It is about the love of God and neighbor, grief about our waywardness, gratitude for the merciful salvation

---

1. Roberts, "Fruit of the Spirit," 10.
2. Ibid.

The Fruit of the Spirit

of our God, humility, compassion, love, and hope.[3] Too often the Christian life centers on the performance of religious activities and duties. While such activities and duties should not be neglected, the focus of a godly life resides in the restoration of those character traits which originally marked the image of God in us.

While these character traits or virtues are at the same time traits of human personality, they are also the fruit of God's personality produced in us by the Spirit as the consequence of dwelling for some years in God's presence and allowing the truth of God's Word to become the directing source of our thinking and acting.[4] Robert C. Roberts expressed it this way:

> The fruits of the Spirit are . . . largely fruits of sustained interaction with God. Just as a child picks up traits more or less simply by dwelling in the presence of her parents, so the Christian develops tenderheartedness, compassion, humility, forgiveness, and hope though the fellowship of the Holy Spirit; that is, by dwelling in the presence of God the Father and Jesus Christ, His Son. And this means, to a very large extent, living in a community of serious believers.[5]

I would therefore argue that a life of godliness entails not only an initial spiritual healing but also focuses on the restoration of our distorted human condition. Godliness or spiritual maturity has to do with the healing of the human spirit as the Holy Spirit produces the virtues of Christ in us. The word *virtue* comes from the Latin word for *man* states Roberts, "and indicates a trait which makes a person manly in the sense of *human*."[6] Thus virtues are character traits which humanize and personalize us and restore our dysfunctional human nature. It is possible, therefore, to view the fruit of the Holy Spirit, as Roberts suggests, as traits of a "fully ripened humanity."[7] I agree, for the healing of the human spirit is

3. Ibid.
4. Ibid.
5. Ibid., 12.
6. Ibid., 11.
7. Ibid., 12.

The Humanity of Christ

simultaneously the restoration of the image of God and restoring humans to *authentic humanness*. In other words, in the restoration of those virtues, mirrored perfectly in Christ, God's original intention for the human creature becomes realized. "Too often," writes Donald Bloesch, "we think of a saint as one who possesses peculiar gifts or lives an eccentric mode of life. But the true saint is extraordinary only in that he or she manifests the ordinary qualities of graciousness and kindness to a superlative degree. The life of this person is unusual not because it is superhuman or angelic but because it is authentically human and uncannily down-to-earth."[8] It is the "extraordinary person," writes Roberts, "who acquires these distinctive marks of humanness. It is rare, and maybe never happens, that a person becomes fully human in this sense"[9] in this life.

We can, however, begin the journey with hope. And what a journey! It is a path filled with promise, the promise of wholeness and freedom—the promise of becoming the kind of person which every human being consciously or unconsciously desires to be. In our era of postmodern thought, with its preoccupation with culturally conditioned truth and with its mistrust of metanarrative, the community of God's people should become the arena for the manifestation of genuine humanity, exhibiting in our daily lives the Christ-like characteristics or virtues that God originally purposed in creating humans. We should say to the world, come in and see what kind of people who are being renewed and observe the power of God's truth restoring broken and distorted persons, making them whole.

On the basis of the atoning-reconciliation and atoning-exchange of Christ, the Christian Church should declare to the world with confidence the unprecedented message of freedom with the words of Jesus,

> Come to me, all you who are weary and burdened and I will give you rest. Take my yoke upon you and learn from me, for I am humble in heart, and you will find

---

8. Bloesch, *Theological Notebook*, 160–70.
9. Roberts, "Fruit of the Spirit," 12.

The Fruit of the Spirit

rest for your souls. For my yoke is easy and my burden is light. (Matt 11:28–30)

Epilogue
Biblical Holiness as a Relational Concept

ANY DISCUSSION OF BIBLICAL holiness must begin where the concept begins—the pages of Old Testament Scripture. It is in the Old Testament that the biblical notion of holiness finds its source and original meaning. The ancient word used to convey the notion of the "holy" was *q-d-sh* from which the Old Testament Hebrew word for holy, *qodesh*, and its cognates (*qadosh* and *qadash*) are derived. This primitive syllabic word reaches back before the formation of the Old Testament Scriptures. It goes back to the earliest origins of a people and their language in the ancient Sumerian civilization of the Mesopotamian valley where our ancient biblical ancestors lived. In comparing the word holy (*q-d-sh*) with equivalent words in the ancient Akkadian and Ugaritic languages of that ancient region, the general consensus of linguistic and religious scholars is that the primary meaning of this primitive root word is, *separation* or *to separate*; hence, *to set apart* as unique; that is, *to withdraw from ordinary use.*[1]

In this ancient context, the word was used to designate phenomena or experiences *different* from normal everyday events. A primary criterion that marked these events and experiences as "*separate*" was the perceived possession of *mysterious power* that, on the one hand, evoked a sense of wonder, fascination, and awe,

---

1. Neill, *Christian Holiness*, 13.

Epilogue

while, on the other hand, produced a sense of fear and terror. Since the Old Testament understanding, both in terminology and basic meaning, grew out of this religious and linguistic conceptual soil, we ask, "In what way did the writers of the Old Testament both retain and transform this primitive notion of the holy?"

Three initial observations can be made. (1) The basic meaning of *holy* as *separation* or *to separate*; hence, *to set apart from ordinary use*, in the sense of *to consecrate* or *to sanctify*, was retained by the biblical writers.[2] The word was used exclusively in religious contexts and stood in direct contrast with the word *chol/hol*, meaning *common* or *profane*. It simply designated or characterized persons, places and things as *holy* or *sacred*, that is, *consecrated* for special use. The biblical tradition retained this concept of consecration and applied it to persons, places, and objects specifically set apart in worship and service to God.[3] (2) The original meaning of the word possessed no implicit ethical or moral content; that is, the notions of ethical righteousness and moral purity that we normally associate with the word *holy* were absent from its primitive meaning. (3) Ethical and moral injunctions were interjected into the biblical tradition when the people of God entered into covenantal relationship with Yahweh, the righteous and holy God. This covenantal relationship required that the people of God reflect in their corporate and personal lives the character of their relationship with this holy God. In addition to these linguistic features, two primary meanings governed the word's actual use; namely, an *identifying use* and a *relational use*.

The Identifying Use

In both the biblical and nonbiblical religious traditions, the word performed an *identifying* function. In nonbiblical religious traditions it designated a realm or sphere distinct from common events and experiences characterized by *mysterious, awesome power*

---

2. Otto, *Idea of the Holy*, 12–13.
3. Neill, *Christian Holiness*, 10–13.

The Humanity of Christ

(*mysterium tremendum*).[4] This descriptor was further characterized by Rudolf Otto as *wholly-other, incomprehensible, giving rise to feelings of fascination, wonder, awe,* and *fear*.

Since the word carried no implicit or explicit moral-ethical content in its original meaning, the word's primary contribution was the insertion into human-religious thought the conceptual notion of *transcendence* as that which is "*wholly other*" or uniquely "*different/separate*." In this context the notion of transcendence conveyed was that of an *immanent-transcendence*. By *immanent-transcendence* is meant the presence of some mysterious power or force, while not external to the universe nevertheless transcends common daily experiences. These uncommon events and experiences were normally associated with the occurrence of unusual naturalistic forces and powers confined within the natural order. Thus, the gods of the early Mesopotamian valley, as with much of the ancient world, were principally sky deities and naturalistic forces.[5]

The writers of the Old Testament Scriptures, however, transform this notion of transcendence. They inserted a *personal element* into the concept that I interpret as *transcending-transcendence*.[6] Here the notion of the holy as that which is *separate* referred to a personal God, not confined to the conditions of time and space, and who controls nature and history from that independent position. Since the ancient notion of the holy was one of pure transcendence, that is, it was not limited by adjectival clarifiers, such as *pure* in the phrase, "pure gold,"[7] the Old Testament writers found it to be a useful and appropriate word for describing the nature of the biblical God. The word, holy, therefore, was co-opted and brought into service to identify the One-and-Only God, whose holiness implied that God has no equals. Thus, to ascribe holiness to God simply meant to identify God's unique transcendence, not in terms of God's moral qualities but in terms of God's personhood

---

4. Otto, *Idea of the Holy*, 12–13.
5. Ibid., 12–44.
6. Eichrodt, *Theology of the Old Testament*, 270.
7. Levine, *Backgrounds for the Bible*, 242.

Epilogue

as the One-and-Only supreme Deity. Exodus 15:11 and Psalm 96:9 provide excellent examples of this use:

> Who is comparable to You among the gods, O Lord? Who is comparable to you—mightiest among the divinities [*ne'dar baqodesh*]? Venerated in hymns of praise, worker of wonders.[8]

Again in Psalm 96:9:

> Worship the Lord in the splendor of his holiness [*bahadrat qodesh*]. Tremble in His presence, all the earth.[9]

The biblical use of the word *holy*, then, identifies the biblical God as singularly unique and absolute among all the claims to deity (Isa 6:3; Ps 89:18; 1 Pet 1:16). Furthermore, of all the attributes ascribed to the divine nature, holiness by virtue of frequency and emphasis occupies a position of singular importance,[10] and also constitutes the source and rationale for the admonition to the people of God to be holy; that is, to give undivided allegiance to this God alone. For "if many gods exist among whom the God of Israel is simple one, each god," then, notes Stephen Neil, "may reasonable appoint his/her own rules to be observed by the deity's worshippers, and these may have a certain validity each in its own spheres."[11] But "if Yahweh is the one true God and all others are no more than idols, the picture undergoes a startling change."[12] To assert, then, that the biblical God was "holy" simply conveyed the notion that God is the One-and-only deity that exists and all other are false. Moreover, it also entailed a total and unqualified demand of worship and honor to this God alone.

As related to the singular unique majesty of God's activity, divine holiness articulates the origin and the manner of the

---

8. Ibid., 251. See also Ps 77:13; Amos 4:2.
9. Levine, *Backgrounds for the Bible*, 250.
10. Eichrodt, *Theology of the Old Testament*, 270.
11. Neill, "Language of Holiness," 28.
12. Ibid.

The Humanity of Christ

relation in which God relates to creation and to humanity.[13] God's holiness is not an attribute which distances God from us; rather, as John Webster writes, "God is holy precisely as the one who in majesty and freedom and sovereign power bends down to us in mercy."[14] As such, holiness is a dimension of God's personal being. It conveys the majesty of God's actions toward us; that is, the mode or manner of God's relation to us.[15] It is, as Webster described it, "majesty in relation."[16]

God's holiness, therefore, is not an "attribute of impersonal mystery," writes Romanian Orthodox theologian Staniloae,[17] but conveys the uniqueness of God as person. It reveals the majestic personhood of the God who, while being unique among the claims to deity, acts toward humankind in his gracious turning as Father, Son and Holy Spirit. "Holiness, [therefore], is not the antithesis of relation," as John Webster explains,

> it does not drive God from the unholy and locks God into absolute pure separateness. Rather, God's holiness is the quality of God's relation to that which is unholy. . . [It] indicates the manner in which the sovereign God relates.[18]

In essence, God's holiness conveys the majesty and the incomparable uniqueness of the One-and-Only God who chooses to encounter the unholy in self-sacrificing love. It reveals the awesomeness of a God who loves us with an incomprehensible love.

A Relational Use

In addition to the *identifying* use that designates the uniqueness of God's nature as the One-and-Only supreme personal deity, a

13. Webster, *Holiness*, 44.
14. Ibid., 45.
15. Ibid., 41.
16. Ibid.
17. Staniloae, *Orthodox Dogmatic Theology*, 223.
18. Webster, *Holiness*, 47.

Epilogue

second, and important, use of the word emerges; namely, a *relational* one. Here the verbal use dominates. In this use the word *holy* signified a process of *consecration* or *purification* whereby persons, places, and objects become *related to* or come to *belong* exclusively to the sacred/holy realm. In non-Christian religions this ancient process of consecration or purification entails a whole array of activities from ritual practices and magical procedures to special sacrifices, anointings, and special incantations, etc., were involved in the attribution of holiness.

The consequence of this consecrating process was the *setting apart* of persons, places and objects from common everyday use to become the exclusive property of the realm of the sacred/holy. Here again no ethical or moral connotations were implicit in the attribution of holiness. Holiness merely denoted that the person or object now belonged exclusively to the sacred-holy realm. The focus, however, was not on the act of separation, but on the fact that the person or object came to belong exclusively to the realm of the *set apart*.[19] Thus "to interpret holy [in its relational use]," writes Norman Snaith, as "*separation from* or to invest the word with inherent ethical-moral content in its original significance is to move away from its central core meaning."[20] This relational use as *belonging to*; that is, *separated to* in an exclusive sense, has important implications for the biblical command to be holy.

HOLINESS AND MORAL-ETHICAL RESPONSIBILITY

Since no ethical-moral content existed in the original *relational* use of the word, when did the biblical imperatives of moral-ethical responsibility before God and toward others become part of the concept of holiness? Did they enter with the command, *not eat of the tree*, given to our ancient ancestors Adam and Eve? Or stated differently, does *obedience* constitute a necessary condition for

---

19. Snaith, *Distinctive Ideas*, 30.
20. Ibid.

The Humanity of Christ

the *belonging-to* holy relationship with God? If not, what, then, is the role of *obedience* in this unique *belonging-to* relationship with God? Consider two contrasting answers.

Moral-Obedience View of Holiness

This view maintains that the divine command, *Thou shall not eat of the tree*, introduced a conditional basis for the *belonging-to* relationship between God and the first human persons. Since commands inherently involve the obligation to obey, the first humans are declared *good* (in a moral sense) by God if-and-only-if they *obey* God's commands. Failure to obey would result not only in separation from fellowship with God but also the loss of original goodness. According to this interpretation, the divine command, *not eat of the tree*, therefore, introduced not only an explicit moral condition for belonging to God, but also constitutes the ground for maintaining the original *goodness* of the human creature. O. Palmer Robertson appears to make this point when he writes,

> The focal point of the covenant [of creation] rested specifically on this single test: "*Do not eat of the tree*." If Adam succeeded in submitting to God at this point, his blessing under the larger provision of the covenant of creation was assured . . . Radical obedience, therefore, provides the key to blessing under the covenant of creation. If man will acknowledge fully the lordship of the Creator by obeying his word purely for the sake of obedience, he shall experience the consummate blessing of the covenant. Life in perpetuity [forever] shall be his.[21]

Did the divine command given in the creation account, then, inserted a special basis for the human creature's status of *belonging to* God? Did it provided an ultimate point of reference in the midst of the Creator's bountiful blessing by which the relationship of *set apart/belonging to* God was to be sustained?

---

21. Robertson, *Christ of the Covenants*, 83.

Epilogue

From this perspective, the original sin of our first ancestors, then, resided in an act of deliberate disobedience to God's command. The consequence was a severed relationship with the Creator and the loss of original goodness. The judgment of God for this original sin, however, was not a divine cataclysm from on high coming down to consume sinful humanity. Rather, God's wrath consisted in *giving them over* (Rom 14, 26, 28); that is, in permitting humanity to have its own way. The divine judgment, writes Paul Achtemeier, was the "withdrawal of the gracious power of God's absolute lordship, allowing other lordships to prevail."[22] In essence, God's judgment on sin was to allow sin to prevail with all its dehumanizing consequences.

God's judgment upon humanity, however, is overwhelmed by God's grace. In an act of unprecedented of grace God enters into the human situation in Jesus Christ. For only the radical obedience of Christ can restore the guilt of the Adam's radical disobedience. Thus, Christ becomes the "second Adam" (1 Cor 15 5–49; 15:21–22; Rom 5:12–19). Through faith in the atoning work of Christ, believers are not only restored back into fellowship with God but are also summoned back to a life of holiness (sanctification); that is, back to doing that which is right, back to walking in obedience to God's commands. In the context of this view, biblical holiness (sanctification), therefore, focuses on placing the human person back under the obligation of obedience, a status that mirrors the original moral-obedient basis between God and our first parents. While the empowering source for this obedience lies in the grace of God in Jesus Christ, believers are, nevertheless (in the context of this view), called to be *obedient-participants* in the actualization of what could be called an *obedient-faith* relationship with God.

Obedient-faith conveys the view that obedience provides the *assurance* or *evidence* of the *faith-belonging to* relationship with God. John MacArthur expressed the point this way, "Clearly no past experience—not even prophesying, casting out demons, or doing signs and wonders—can be viewed as evidence of salvation [belonging to God] apart from a life of obedience . . . Faith that

---

22. Achtemeier, *Romans*, 40.

The Humanity of Christ

does not result in righteous living is dead and cannot save."[23] Jerry Bridges makes similar emphasis when he writes, "Obedience is the pathway to holiness . . . It is clear from this passage ['put to death the misdeeds of the body,' Rom 8:13] that God puts responsibility to living a holy life squarely on us. We re to do something . . . We need to brace ourselves up, and to realize that we are responsible for our thoughts, attitudes, and actions."[24]

While this view clearly maintains that salvation is entirely by grace, the position nevertheless asserts that the *assurance* of the faith-relationship is found in the fruit of obedience. Where there is no fruit of discipleship, where there is no obedience to God's Word, there is no assurance that one *belongs to* God. Holiness of life, therefore, centers predominately on obedience in conformity to the standards of conduct prescribed by God. It is in essence the pursuit of godliness by means of obedience.

While this interpretation faces several difficulties, I will note only two. First, the divine declaration of *goodness* ("It is good," Gen 1:28–32) attributed to the first humans should not be taken as a *moral* declaration. This is evident from the fact that the same declaration of *goodness* is applied to animals and other creative acts (Gen 1:11, 12, 18, 25, 31). Since animals by nature are amoral creatures that simply function in harmony with the deterministically designed nature given by God, the original affirmation of human *goodness* conveys a purpose other than a moral one conditioned by obedience.

Second, the original act of disobedience was motivated by a state prior to the act; namely, the emergence of a heart of distrust. This emergence of unbelief prior to the *act* of disobedience was initiated by the introduction of an alternative promise, "You will not die," that brought into question the trustworthiness of God's command. Believing that they (Adam/Eve) would *not die* but would be "like God, knowing good and evil," Adam (Eve) rejected God's command and chose to put their trust in the alternative word. Hence, the act of disobedience was not merely the breaking

---

23. MacArthur, *Gospel according to Jesus*, 22–23.
24. Bridges, *Pursuit of Holiness*, 82, 84.

Epilogue

of God's law but (and critically sense) the breaking of a trust relationship with God.[25] Since it is theoretically possible to envision a situation in which overt acts of disobedience are absent from our lives and yet be consciously aware that sin is still present in evil attitudes and lustful desires, the deduction is made that sin begins first in the heart/mind before it occurs in overt acts of disobedience. This is why holiness, in my opinion, cannot be achieved simply by means of the imposition upon believers of an arbitrary plan or standard of behavior, even if these standards of conduct are of an ideological or religious nature.[26]

The Functional View of Holiness

In contrast with the "Moral-Obedient View," I propose an alternative interpretation, entitled the "Functional View" of holiness. This view advances the premise that the first humans, having been created *good* and endowed with the capacity of *personal being* (in God's image), should *function* (think and act) in a manner harmonious with the human nature given by God, thereby reflecting the character of God in whose image the humans were created.

The biblical text records God's delight in the functional nature of the first humans with the words, *It is good* (Gen 1:31). But what precisely is the *good* for which the human creature was created?[27] The *good* for which the human was created resides in the capacity for *personal relatedness* that in depth and complexity functions beyond the capability of our nearest fellow creatures.[28] This God-given capacity finds exposition in the negatively expressed biblical statement, *It is not good for man to be alone* (Gen 2:18). This statement is not referring to the emotional experience of *loneliness*, but rather to the fact that Adam's solitary state was not good. The underlying premise is: God cannot create a solitary

---

25. Bloesch, *Theological Notebook*, 46.
26. Anderson and Guernsey, *On Being Family*, 117.
27. Neill, *Christian Holiness*, 16.
28. Ibid.

The Humanity of Christ

being and simultaneously declare this being to be in the divine image. In other words, the human creature, writes Stephen Neill, "cannot realize, in solitary communion with him [her] self, that which he [she] has in him [her] self to be; he [she] can realize it only . . . in fellowship with the other."[29] The *good*, then, for which the human was created by God, is a *good* that is realized only in fellowship with God and other reciprocal beings.[30]

This personal-relational capacity was functionally inaugurated with the creation of the woman (Eve). The creation of the woman constitutes an essential component in God's vision and purpose of an I-Thou (communal) relational experience within humanity. An I-Thou relationship requires a being capable of reciprocity.

With the creation of the woman an encounter or meeting is made possible that manifests a remarkable unity within diversity that mirrors the interactive communion within the Trinitarian nature of God.[31] This relational capacity, moreover, constitutes the uniqueness of the human creature as created in the image of God.

HOLINESS AS A RELATIONAL CONCEPT

Holiness, therefore, does not reside in some private or inner consecration; it is primarily a matter of relationship—first with the One who created the human creature, but this involves also right relations with others reciprocal beings.[32] Since God relates to the created world out of divine wisdom and love, so human creatures possesses the same capacities in their earthly reality because humans were created in the divine image. While the image of God in the human person includes the human's peculiar relationship to God as God's vice-regent on earth, the image more specially constitutes the human's capacity to mirror in his/her thinking

---

29. Ibid., 16–17.
30. Anderson, *On Being Human*, 16.
31. Ibid., 105.
32. Neil, *Christian Holiness*, 17.

Epilogue

and acting the character of God in the same analogous manner that a child reflects in his/her thinking and acting the image of his/her parents.[33] "Just as God in the perfection of His character was creating the world in wisdom and loving care for man [humans]," contends LaRondelle, "so [humans are] made and called to make manifest and develop that divine character as his [her] own in earthly reality, because he/[she] is the [child] of this Father Creator."[34]

The image of God, therefore, is not essentially a doctrine about the possession of certain human attributes, such as reason, though such attributes contribute to the expression of humanness, but resides more specifically in the human's capacity for personal-relational encounters both with God and others. "Just as the Creator," writes LaRondelle, "who crowned [the human creature] with glory and honor, [and] praise as functioning 'completely perfect' [hence, 'good'] [thus, the human creature] is called to follow and imitate God and to join all creation in proclaiming the glory of God and praising the beauty and majesty of the perfection of God's character."[35] The image of God, therefore, entails a responsibility and a task "to reflect and honor in our character and life, in our authority and dominion over the earth, the very character of our Maker."[36]

To argue that humans are called to mirror the moral-spiritual character of God, however, is not intended to diminish the fact that humans are simultaneously creaturely beings. Human creatureliness is the broad field upon which the occasion of the uniqueness of human nature occurs.[37] As humans, we possess creaturely life; that is, we are, in an essential way, biological beings. We share an inescapable bond with all creatures that possess the breath of life. Nevertheless, humans experience what Ray S. Anderson calls, a

---

33. LaRondelle, *Perfection and Perfectionism*, 63–64.
34. Ibid., 64.
35. Ibid., 68.
36. Ibid.
37. Anderson, *On Being Human*, 21.

The Humanity of Christ

double jeopardy of existence by virtue of being human.[38] In other words, the purpose of human existence is not achieved simply by virtue of sustaining creaturely life. While nonhuman creatures have nothing to lose in being no more than their creaturely nature allows them to be, humans have a *destiny*, while dependent upon creaturely survival, reaches for more than creatureliness can give."[39] Human existence, therefore, possesses a calling and goal to which nonhuman creatures are not bound.

This destiny is bound up with the possession of a spiritual dimension (orientation) created by the divine Word, the Word by which the human creature is called out of the deterministic cycle of nature and into fellowship with the God the Creator. This is a life and fellowship to which no other creature is summoned. This spiritual dimension—this capacity to reflect the moral-spiritual character of God, constitutes not only the core of the biblical admonition to be holy as God is holy but also reveals the *analogia entis* between God and the human creature created in the divine image. As God is essentially a relational being, revealed in the nature of God's Trinitarian personhood, the human creature also possesses a relational capacity as the consequence of the possession of the *human spirit*. While not divorced from creaturely existence, this self-relational capacity of the spirit, nevertheless, reaches beyond the deterministically conditionedness of human creatureliness, and enables encounters of self-giving love, empathy, kindness, patience, artistic creativity, etc., and, most specifically, relational encounters with God. It is this relational capacity, enabled by the *human spirit* that not only marks the human in the *divine image* but also functions as the indispensable source for I-Thou encounters by which humans engage in relationship both with God and other reciprocal beings.

If humans were created with an integrity of their own within the contingent order of creation as a gift of divine love and grace,[40] it is logical to assume, then, that salvation would involve not only

---

38. Ibid., 115.
39. Ibid.
40. Torrance, *Trinitarian Faith*, 90–91.

Epilogue

reconciliation with God but also the restoration of that integrity so that humans may once again function according to the purpose for which God created them. This implies, then, that holiness is not simply a religious task, but also a human one; that is, by God's grace and our continued response to that grace we might be restored back to thinking and acting according to the purpose for which God created us in the divine image. The evidence of this restoration resides in the manifestation of those virtues or character traits that are biblical designated as the "fruit of the Spirit."

Bibliography

Achtemeier, Paul. *Romans*. Interpretation. Atlanta: John Knox, 1985.
Alexander, Donald. *Christian Spirituality: Five Views of Sanctification*. Downers Grove: InterVarsity, 1988.
———. *The Pursuit of Godliness: Sanctification in Christological Perspective*. Lanham: University Press of America, 1999.
Anderson, Ray S. *Ministry on the Fireline: A Practical Theology for an Empowered Church*. Downers Grove: InterVarsity, 1993.
———. *On Being Human: Essays in Theological Anthropology*. Grand Rapids: Eerdmans, 1982.
Anderson, Ray S., and Dennis B. Guernsey, eds. *On Being Family*. Grand Rapids: Eerdmans, 1985.
Augustine. *Basic Writings of Saint Augustine*. Vol. 1. Edited by Whitney J. Oates. Translated by J. G. Pilkington. New York: Random House, 1946.
Barth, Karl. *The Doctrine of Creation*. Part 4. Vol. 3.2 of *Church Dogmatics*. Edinburgh: T. & T. Clark, 1936–1962.
———. *The Humanity of God*. Atlanta: John Knox, 1976.
Beilby, James K., and Paul Rhodes Eddy, eds. *Justification: Five Views*. Downers Grove: IVP Academic, 2011.
Blocher, Henri. *Original Sin: Illuminating the Riddle*. Downers Grove: InterVarsity, 1997.
Bloesch, Donald G. *Theological Notebook*. Vol. 1. Colorado Springs: Helmers & Howard, 1989.
Braaten, Carl E., and Philip Clayton, eds. *The Theology of Wolfhart Pannenberg*. Minneapolis: Augsburg, 1988.
Bridges, Jerry. *The Pursuit of Holiness*. Colorado Springs: NavPress, 1978.
Brown, Warren S., et al., eds. *Whatever Happened to the Soul? Scientific and Theological Portraits of Human Nature*. Minneapolis: Fortress, 1998.
Brown, William P. *Character in Crisis*. Grand Rapids: Eerdmans, 1996.
Calvin, John. *The Institutes of the Christian Religion*. Edited by John T. McNeill and translated by Ford Lewis Battles. Library of Christian Classics 10. Philadelphia: Westminster, 1960.

Bibliography

Carmichael, Kay. *Sin and Forgiveness: New Responses in a Changing World*. Burlington: Ashgate, 2003.

Charry, Ellen T. *By the Renewing of Your Minds: The Pastoral Function of Christian Doctrine*. Oxford: Oxford University Press, 1997.

Christensen, Michael J., and Jeffery A. Wittung. *Partakers of the Divine Nature: The History and Development of Deification in the Christian Tradition*. Grand Rapids: Baker Academic, 2007.

Cohen, Marc S., et al., eds. *Readings in Ancient Greek Philosophy: From Thales to Aristotle*. Rev. ed. Indianapolis: Hackett, 2011.

Colyer, Elmer M. *How to Read T. F. Torrance: Understanding His Trinitarian & Scientific Theology*. Downers Grove: InterVarsity, 2001.

Come, Arnold B. *Human Spirit and Holy Spirit*. Philadelphia: Westminster, 1959.

Crabtree, Harriet. *The Christian Life: Traditional Metaphors and Contemporary Theologies*. Harvard Dissertations in Religion. Minneapolis: Fortress, 1991.

Curtis, Edward M., and John J. Brugaletta. *Discovering the Way of Wisdom: Spirituality in the Wisdom Literature*. Grand Rapids: Kregal, 2004.

Chryssavgis, John. "Original Sin: An Orthodox Perspective." In *Grace and Disgrace: A Theology of Self-Esteem, Society, and History*, edited by Neil Ormerod, 197–206. Newtown, Australia: Dwyer, 1992.

Danker, Frederick William. *The Greek-English Lexicon of the New Testament*. Chicago: University of Chicago Press, 1979.

Dayton, Wilber T. "Entire Sanctification: The Divine Purification and Perfection of Man." In *A Contemporary Wesleyan Theology: Biblical, Systematic Theology, and Practical*, edited by Charles W. Carter, 1:517–69. Grand Rapids: Francis Asbury, 1983.

Dockery, D. S. "New Nature and Old Nature." In *Dictionary of Paul and His Letters*, edited by Gerald F. Hawthorne et al., 628–29. Downers Grove: InterVarsity, 1992.

Durant, Will. *The Story of Philosophy*. New York: Simon & Schuster, 1929.

Eichrodt, Walther. *Theology of the Old Testament*. Vol. 1. Philadelphia: Westminster, 1961.

Erickson, Millard. *Christian Theology*. Vol. 3. Grand Rapids: Baker Book House, 1983.

Evans, C. Stephen. *Soren Kierkegaard's Christian Psychology*. Vancouver: Regent College Publishing, 1990.

Fee, Gordon. *God's Empowering Presence: The Holy Spirit in the Letters of Paul*. Peabody, MA: Hendrickson, 1994.

Forde, Gerhard O. "Forensic Justification and the Law in Lutheran Theology." In *Justification by Faith: Lutheran and Catholics in Dialogue VII*, edited by H. George Anderson et al., 278–303. Minneapolis: Augsburg, 1985.

———. "The Lutheran View." In *Christian Spirituality: Five Views*, edited by Donald L. Alexander, 13–32. Grand Rapids: InterVarsity, 1988.

Bibliography

Foster, Roger T., and Paul V. Marston. *God's Strategy in Human History*. Bromley, UK: Send the Light Trust, 1973.

Fryling, Robert A. *The Leadership Ellipse: Shaping How We Lead by Who We Are*. Downers Grove: InterVarsity, 2010.

Gammie, John G. *Holiness in Israel*. Minneapolis: Fortress, 1989.

Grenz, Stanley J., and Roger E. Olson. *20th Century Theology: God & the World in a Transitional Age*. Downers Grove: InterVarsity, 1992.

Grey, Mary. "Falling into Freedom: New Images of Sin in Contemporary Society." *Scottish Journal of Theology* 47 (1940) 223–44.

Grudem, Wayne. *Systematic Theology*. Downers Grove: InterVarsity, 1994.

Hendry, George S. *The Holy Spirit in Christian Theology*. Rev. ed. Philadelphia: Westminster, 1956.

Jeeves, Malcolm. *Minds, Brains, Souls and Gods: A Conversation on Faith, Psychology and Neuroscience*. Grand Rapids: InterVarsity, 2013.

Jeeves, Malcolm, and Warren S. Brown. *Neuroscience, Psychology and Religion*. West Conshohocken, PA: Templeton, 2009.

Jewett, Paul, and Marguerite Shuster. *Who We Are: Our Dignity as Human*. Grand Rapids: Eerdmans, 1996.

Kidner, Derek. *The Message of Ecclesiastes: A Time to Mourn and a Time to Dance*. Downers Grove: InterVarsity, 1976.

Kierkegaard, Soren. *The Sickness unto Death*. Translated by Alastair Hannay. London: Penguin, 1989.

Konig, Adrio. *Here Am I! A Christian Reflection on God*. Grand Rapids: Eerdmans, 1982.

Kunneth, Walter. *The Theology of the Resurrection*. Translated by James W. Leitch. St. Louis: Concordia, 1965.

LaRondelle, Hans Karl. *Perfection and Perfectionism: A Dogmatic-Ethical Study of Biblical Perfection and Phenomenal Perfectionism*. Berrien Springs, MI: Andrews University Press, 1975.

Legge, James, trans. *The Four Books: Analects of Confuciasm*. Changsha: Hunan, 1995.

Levine, Baruch. "The Language of Holiness: Perceptions of the Sacred in the Hebrew Bible." In *Backgrounds for the Bible*, edited by Michael Patrick O'Conner and David Joel Freedman, 241–52. Winona Lake: Eisenbrauns, 1987.

Livingston, James C., and Francis Schussler Fiorenza. *Modern Christian Thought*. Vols. 1 and 2, *The Twentieth Century*. Upper Saddle River, NJ: Prentice Hall, 2000.

Loder, James E. *The Logic of the Spirit: Human Development in Theological Perspective*. San Francisco: Jossey-Bass, 1998.

———. *The Transforming Moment*. Colorado Springs: Helmers & Howard, 1989.

Loder, James E., and W. Jim Neidhardt. *The Knight's Move: The Relational Logic of the Spirit in Theology and Science*. Colorado Springs: Helmers & Howard, 1992.

Bibliography

Long, A. A., ed. *The Cambridge Companion to Early Greek Philosophy*. Cambridge: Cambridge University Press, 1999.

Loomer, Bernard. "Two Conceptions of Power." *Process Studies* 6 (1976) 5–32.

MacArthur, John. *The Gospel according to Jesus*. Grand Rapids: Zondervan, 1988.

Maximus the Confessor. *Photus Library*. Edited by R. Henry. Paris: Belle Letters, 1960.

Meyendorff, John. *Byzantine Theology: Historical Trends & Doctrinal Themes*. New York: Fordham University Press, 1974.

Moody, Dale. *The Word of Truth*. Grand Rapids: Eerdmans, 1981.

Moore, Hyatt. *In the Image of God: Faces and Souls That Reflect Their Creator*. Orlando: Wycliffe, 1999.

Moreland, J. P., and Scott B. Rae. *Body and Soul: Human Nature and the Crisis in Ethics*. Downers Grove: InterVarsity, 2000.

Morris, Leon. *Testaments of Love: A Study of Love in the Bible*. Grand Rapids: Eerdmans, 1981.

Murphy, Nancey C., and Warren S. Brown. *Did My Neurons Make Me Do It? Philosophical and Neurobiological Perspective on Moral Responsibility and Free Will*. Oxford: Oxford University Press, 2007.

Neill, Stephen. *Christian Holiness*. New York: Harper & Row, 1960.

———. "The Language of Holiness: Perceptions of the Sacred in the Hebrew Bible." In *Backgrounds for the Bible*, edited by Michael Patrick O'Connor and David Noel Freedman, 241–52. Winona Lake: Eisenbrauns, 1987.

Newbigin, Lesslie. *The Open Secret*. Rev. ed. Grand Rapids: Eerdmans, 1995.

Niebuhr, Reinhold. *The Nature and Destiny of Man*. Vol. 1, *Human Nature*. New York: Scribner, 1941.

Niebuhr, Richard R. *Schleiermacher on Christ and Religion: A New Introduction*. New York: Scribner, 1964.

Olson, Roger. "Pannenberg's Theological Anthropology: A Review Article." *Scottish Journal of Theology* 36 (1986).

Otto, Rudolf. *The Idea of the Holy*. Translated by John W. Harvey. London: Oxford University Press, 1970.

Ormerod, Neil. *Grace and Disgrace: A Theology of Self-Esteem, Society, and History*. E. J. Dwyer, Newtown, Australia, 1992.

Outler, Albert C. "The Loss of the Sacred." *Christianity Today*, January 2, 1981.

Pannenberg, Wolfhart. *Anthropology in Theological Perspective*. Translated by Matthew J. O'Connnell. Philadelphia: Westminster, 1985.

———. *Christian Spirituality*. Philadelphia: Westminster, 1983.

———. *What Is Man?* Translated by Duane A. Priebe. Philadelphia: Fortress, 1970.

Patterson, Bob. E. *Reinhold Niebuhr: Makers of the Modern Theological Mind*. Waco: Word, 1977.

Payton, James R., Jr. *Light from the Christian East: An Introduction to the Orthodox Tradition*. Downers Grove: InterVarsity, 2007.

Bibliography

Pringle-Pattison, A. Seth. *The Idea of God in the Light of Recent Philosophy*. Oxford: Oxford University Press, 1920.

Reardon, Bernard M. G. *Religious Thought in the Nineteenth Century*. Cambridge, Cambridge University Press, 1966.

Reardon, Patrick Henry. *The Jesus We Missed*. Nashville: Thomas Nelson, 2012.

Roberts, Robert C. "Fruit of the Spirit." *Reformed Journal*, February 1987, 9–13.

———. *Spirituality and Human Emotion*. Grand Rapids: Eerdmans, 1982.

Robertson, O. Palmer. *The Christ of the Covenants*. Grand Rapids: Baker, 1989.

Russell, Norman. *The Doctrine of Deification in the Greek Patristic Tradition*. Oxford: Oxford University Press, 2004.

Russell, Walter. "The Apostle Paul's View of the 'Sin Nature'-'New Nature' Struggle." In *Christian Perspectives on Being Human*, edited by J. P. Moreland and David M. Ciocchi, 207–27. Grand Rapids: Baker, 1993.

Schleiermacher, Friedrich. *On Christian Faith*. Vol. 1. Edited by H. R. Mackintosh and J. S. Stewart. New York: Harper & Row, 1963.

Sherlock, Charles. *The Doctrine of Humanity: Contours of Christian Theology*. Downers Grove: InterVarsity, 1996.

Shults, F. LeRon. *Reforming Theological Anthropology: After the Philosophical Turn to Relationality*. Grand Rapids: Eerdmans, 2003.

Smith, John. *Reason and God: Encounters of Philosophy with Religion*. New Haven: Yale University Press, 1961.

Snaith, Norman. *Distinctive Ideas of the Old Testament*. London: Epworth, 1944.

Snodgrass, Klyne. "Spheres of Influence." *Journal for the Study of the New Testament* 32 (1988) 93–113.

Staniloae, Dumitru. *Orthodox Dogmatic Theology*. Vol. 1, *Revelation and Knowledge of the Triune God: The Experience of God*. Brookline, MA: Holy Cross Orthodox Press, 1994.

Suchocki, Marjorie Hewitt. *The Fall to Violence: Original Sin in Relational Theology*. New York: Continuum International, 1995.

Tennant, Frederick R. *The Origin and Propagation of Sin*. Reprint. Lexon, MA: Hardpress, 2012.

———. *Philosophical Theology*. Vol. 1, *The Soul and Its Faculties*. Reprint. Cambridge: Cambridge University Press, 1968.

———. *Philosophical Theology*. Vol. 2, *The World, the Soul, and God*. Reprint. Cambridge: Cambridge University Press, 1968.

———. *The Source of the Doctrines of the Fall and Original Sin*. Cambridge: Cambridge University Press, 2012.

Torrance, Robert M. *The Spiritual Quest*. Berkeley: University of California Press, 1994.

Torrance, T. F. *The Christian Doctrine of God: One Being Three Persons*. Edinburgh: T. & T. Clark, 1997.

———. *The Christian Frame of Mind: Reason, Order, and Openness in Theology and Natural Science*. Colorado Springs: Helmers & Howard, 1989.

———. "Goodness and Dignity of Man in the Christian Tradition." With Elmer M. Colyer. *Modern Theology* 5 (1988) 309–22.

Bibliography

———. *The Mediation of Christ*. Colorado Springs: Helmers & Howard, 1992.

———. "Soul and Person in Theological Perspective." In *Religion, Reason, and the Self: Essays in Honour of Hywel D. Lewis*, with Elmer M. Colyer, edited by Stewart E. Sutherland and T. A. Roberts, 10–118. Cardiff: University of Wales Press, 1989. ———. *Trinitarian Faith: The Evangelical Theology of the Ancient Catholic Church*. Edinburgh: T. & T. Clark, 1988.

Trevarthen, Colwyn, ed. *Brain Circuits and Functions of the Mind: Essays in Honor of Roger W. Sperry*. Cambridge: Cambridge University Press, 1990.

Walton, John. *The Lost World of Adam and Eve: Genesis 2–3 and the Human Origins Debate*. Downers Grove: InterVarsity, 2015.

Ware, Timothy. *The Orthodox Church*. Reprint. New York: Penguin, 1969.

Webster, John. *Holiness*. Grand Rapids: Eerdmans, 2003.

Weinandy, Thomas. *In the Likeness of Sinful Flesh*. Edinburgh: T. & T. Clark, 1993.

Welker, Michael. *God the Spirit*. Translated by John Hoffmeyer. Minneapolis: Fortress, 1994.

Yong, Amos. *Discerning the Spirit(s): A Pentecostal-Charismatic Contribution to Christian Theology of Religions*. Sheffield, UK: Sheffield Academic, 2000.

Index of Authors

Achtemeier, Paul, 22, 83, 84, 117
Alexander, Donald L., 31
Anderson, Ray S., 6, 7, 12, 35, 49, 81, 82, 92, 119, 120, 121, 122
Augustine of Hippo, 85

Barth, Karl, 15, 21, 47, 81
Blocher, Henri, 63, 65, 66, 67, 68
Bloesch, Donald G., 67, 108, 119
Bridges, Jerry, 118
Brown, Warren S., 2, 3

Calvin, John, 43, 59
Carmichael, Kay, 49
Charry, Ellen T., 81
Colyer, Elmer M., 25, 26, 91, 93
Chryssavgis, John, 24, 25

Danker, Frederick William, 94
Dockery D. S., 72
Durant, Will, 86

Eichrodt, Walther, 112, 113
Erickson, Millard, 64
Evans, C. Stephen, 32, 33, 36, 74
Fee, Gordon, 71

Gregory of Nazianius, 18
Grey, May, 73
Grudem, Wayne, 59

Hendry, George S., 41, 42, 43, 44, 45

Jeeves, Malcolm, 82, 83
Jewett, Paul, 13

Karkkainen, Veli-Matti, 21
Kidner, Derek, 14, 15
Kierkegaard, Soren, 30, 32, 32
Konig, Adrio, 91, 92
Kunneth, Walter, 97

Legge, James, 33
LaRondelle, Hans K., 121
Levine, Baruch, 20, 112, 113
Livingston, James C., 54
Loder, James E., 16, 22, 30, 33, 34, 37, 38, 45, 73, 88, 91
Loomer, Bernard, 100–102
Luther, Martin, 43

MacArthur, John, 117
Maximus the Confessor: 76
Meyendorff, John, 23, 24, 69, 76
Moody, Dale, 50
Moore, Hyatt, xiii, 17
Morris, Leon, 92
Murphy, Nancy C., 1

Neill, Stephen, 110, 111, 113, 119, 120
Newbigin, Lesslie, 19, 120

Index of Authors

Niebuhr, Reinhold, 54, 55
Niebuhr, Richard R., 55

Otto, Rudolf, 111, 112
Olson, Roger E., 37, 38
Outler, Albert C., 49, 85, 86

Pannenberg, Wolfhard, 4, 13, 37
Pringle-Pattison, Seth, 41

Roberts, Robert C., 106–8
Robertson, O. Palmer, 65, 116
Russell, Walter, 71, 72

Schleiermacher, Friedrich, 51, 52, 53
Snaith, Norman, 57, 115

Snodgrass, Klyne, 4
Staniloae, Dumitru, 114
Suchocki, Marjorie Hewitt, 75

Tennant, Frederick R., 51.
Torrance, Robert M., 32, 85
Torrance, Thomas F., 21, 22, 25, 26, 27, 39, 40, 41, 46, 75, 84, 85, 87, 90, 91, 122

Walton, John, 67
Webster, John, 114
Weinandy, Thomas, 16, 26
Welker, Michael, 8, 9, 10, 11

Yong, Amos, 19.

Index of Subjects

Agent of Transformational Change, 21, 22
Alexander, Donald, 31, 61–64
Anderson, Ray S., 6, 7, 12, 35, 49 81, 82, 92, 119, 120, 122
Atoning Exchange, 25, 26, 27, 28
Authentic Personhood, 86, 98
Augustine, 58–61

Barth, Karl, 15, 47, 28, 81
Brown, Warren, 1–4
Calvin, John, 58–61
Colyer, Elmer M, 25, 26, 91, 93
Community (Persons-in-community): 5, 8, 17–20
Chryssavgis, John, 24–25

Defining the Human Spirit, x. xii, 3, 30, 47
Dysfunction of human spirit, 22, 23, 48, 50, 84

Evans, C. Stephen, 32, 33, 36, 74
Fee, Gordon, 71
Flesh vs Spirit, 70, 75, 76, 85
Freedom of the Divine Spirit, 75, 83
Fruit of the Divine Spirit, 25, 106–8

Goal of Redemption, xii, 8, 9
Gray, Mary, 73

Gruden, Wayne, 59

Henry, George, 42, 45, 47
Holiness of God, 112–14
Holy—Linguistic origin & Use, 110–11
Holy—relational concept, 110, 114, 115, 120–23
Human Personhood & image of God, xii, 8, 9
Human Spirituality, 82, 86
Humanity of Christ, 25, 28, 30
Human spirit, 1–4, 19, 82, 83
Human Soul, 1–11, 15, 78

Interpretations of sin, 50–64
Incarnation, 92–94, 94–99
Image of God, 78

Jeeves, Malcolm, 82, 83
Jewett, Paul, 13

Kierkegaard, Soren, 30, 33, 37

Loder, James, 16, 18, 22, 30, 33 34, 37, 38, 45, 73, 88
Love of God, 90–92
Luther, Martin, 43
Levine, Baruch, 20, 112–13

Moore, Hyatt, xiii, xiv

Index of Subjects

Obedience (Function), 65–67, 115–16, 118, 119–23
Ontological Aloneness, 84
Origin of sin, 68–70, 71, 74, 80, 81
Outler, Albert, 95, 86

Pannenberg, Wolfhart, 5–6, 37–38
Power of love, 90. 92

Relationality (Concept), 1–4, 17–19, 24, 25
Regeneration, 25, 27, 85, 89
Redemption, 5, 6, 97
Resurrection, 97

Roberts, Robert C., 106–8
Robertson, O. Palmer, 65, 116

Sinful Nature, xii, 4, 5, 70–72

Tennant, F. R., 52
Torrance, Thomas F., 21, 22. 25–27, 39, 40–42, 46, 75, 84, 85, 87, 90–91, 122
Torrance, Robert 31, 84, 85

Vicarious Human, 25, 26, 28, 95

Welker, John, 8–11, 13, 17–20

www.ingramcontent.com/pod-product-compliance
Lightning Source LLC
Chambersburg PA
CBHW051943160426
43198CB00013B/2279